Dynamic
Police
Training

Dynamic Police Training

Ann R. Bumbak

CRC Press
Taylor & Francis Group
Boca Raton   London   New York

CRC Press is an imprint of the
Taylor & Francis Group, an **informa** business

CRC Press
Taylor & Francis Group
6000 Broken Sound Parkway NW, Suite 300
Boca Raton, FL 33487-2742

International Standard Book Number: 978-1-4398-1587-8 (Paperback)

Library of Congress Cataloging-in-Publication Data

Bumbak, Ann R.
    Dynamic police training / Ann R. Bumbak.
        p. cm.
    Includes bibliographical references and index.
    ISBN 978-1-4398-1587-8 (pbk. : alk. paper)
    1. Police training. I. Title.

HV7923.B796 2011
363.2'2--dc22

2010025070

This book is dedicated to the memory of my dear friend Lee Edward Goldman, deputy director of the Maryland Police and Correctional Training Commissions and a former sergeant with the Howard County Police Department. May his tireless work for improving police training programs continue to inspire many generations to come.

Table of Contents

Preface

In my heart of hearts, I truly love the profession of law enforcement. Of course, the job itself is exciting, but it is the true sense of brotherhood that keeps us committed to the job over the course of many years. The ranks of police officers, trainers, and supervisors alike are filled with the most conscientious modern-day warriors of our day.

The ancient Roman legions had a deep understanding of the principles of loyalty, courage, and commitment in their time. Historians called this quality *romanitas* (translated literally as Rome-ness). This fundamental propensity lives on in police officers today; it could be referred to as *policitas*. It is this "police-ness," a dignified sense of duty and honor with which police officers operate, that makes working in the profession so worthwhile. Although society often takes a cynical view of cops, I would not trade a single day of my experience with my friends and colleagues on the streets and in the classroom. I know that most, if not all, law enforcement officers feel the same way.

My sole intention when I began to write this book was to offer the final fruition of my experiences in training, in the hopes of paving the path for others in the years to come. Training police officers is not an easy job. It is a completely different position within the toughest job in the world. I personally stumbled along for a number of years, much to the chagrin of my students, in my search for quality instructional delivery. In fact, the idea of writing this book originated with my work in the instructor development program for the State of Maryland's police and correctional officers training venue, beginning in 2008. My supervisor, Mr. Lee Goldman, tasked me with analyzing the content and delivery of our current program for instructor development. His directive was clear: make whatever changes were needed to achieve the results we agreed upon.

As I began to educate myself about how the concepts of instructional system design were traditionally taught, I began to see tremendous opportunities for changing the paradigms of these skills in the profession of law enforcement. As I talked with my students and learned more about their personalities, I saw many parallels in the temperament and preferences of police students. I soon realized that, unsurprisingly, the passive approach of lecture was universally hated by students in our line of work. Yet, how could classroom learning be made more active? I did not know what the alternatives were or how to use them.

I was no expert in the science of the educational process. In fact, I had no formal understanding of curriculum development and primarily relied on instincts and lecture myself when I began my own work as a trainer of police in 1999. I was soon immersed in the writings of adult educators, a field that was far from my own practical experience. I had worked as an adjunct professor, police officer, and field trainer, as well as in an undercover law enforcement role, but I had never studied the educational "heavy hitters" like Bloom or his cohorts. In other words, perhaps I could "run and gun" with the best, but this did not mean that I could effectively train fellow trainers in the ways and means of classroom instruction methods. I think this fundamental ignorance reflects the experience of most people in the field of police training today. This is not an insult to trainers but merely an observation. Police trainers have not had much use for traditional education models because, for our purposes, they are not effective *in practice*. Theories are interesting but not very useful for a profession that requires action, not reflection.

For the first time in my professional life, I forced myself to resist lecture- and slide show-based teaching. I unexpectedly discovered that carefully planned, active learning could be a fun, intellectual, and valid method of teaching. I saw myself in the surprising position of being able to translate these concepts into an understandable language for police trainers. Using games, simulations, and role-playing, my students virtually taught themselves, and I assumed the role of mere facilitator for their own journey. As I watched with great pride, my instructor students came alive using these methods. I began to wonder how I could reach more people with these simple ideas.

During the months I devoted to writing, I found that my own experiences in training, as a law enforcement student over the course of many years in a variety of settings, offered a rare and coherent glimpse of the challenges of training police officers, in particular. These many experiences as a student provided me with additional insight into what works and what does not with our unique audience. It seemed natural to start with the beginning, giving a fifty-mile-high view of police training and field training as a whole, then zooming in for a closer look at the various aspects of the complicated training process that is required to create a competent police officer.

I felt that my readers would also enjoy a straightforward, common-sense discourse on the different domains of learning, simplified for our police-oriented purposes. Thus, the complex cognitive, affective, and psychomotor areas are distilled into the simple "head," "heart," and "hands" examples. The often muddy, hierarchical levels of Bloom's taxonomy are now hopefully illustrated with crystallized, real-world examples that illuminate the importance of training to the right echelon of difficulty for the students.

The realization of a long-held dream is contained within the pages of this book. It is my sincere hope that it will be of some value to a small group of trainers who are ready to implement changes in their traditional training programs. Any wrongful indictment of police training as a whole, misplaced criticism of methods, poor articulation, or off-base accusation I might have made in the name of improving programs is my error alone. I encourage you to note my mistakes and contact me with your feedback. I am always available to you, the peer community of trainers, and pleased to provide any support I can to your developing training programs.

The writing of any book is an exercise in trepidation, even for the most confident author. Publishing is a risky business. In my case, the potential rewards to be reaped for the field seemed worth the personal and professional risk involved. I hope that you will find that you agree with my decision, in the end. With your help, I can continue to learn even more about our universal experience in the position of archetypal classroom leaders, as the educators of the next generation of cops.

Contact me with your comments and suggestions via e-mail at abumbak@yahoo.com.

Acknowledgments

Without the input and inspiration of dozens of professionals, both within and outside of the field of law enforcement, this finished work would not have been possible. I would like to thank some of the people behind the scenes who have made the book you hold in your hands an accomplished vision, as imperfect as it may be.

It has been a rare gift to be able to learn from some of the best police instructors in the business. I credit these inspired, unflappable masters for the memorable and meaningful career I was privileged to spend in law enforcement. For all of the police students who have trusted me with their education over the years, I offer this: It has been my honor to call you my friends and colleagues. The years I have spent in the classroom represent the greatest achievement of my professional life. If I have taught you anything of value, I hope it was a worthwhile investment of your time, and I was grateful for the opportunity. When I fell short, you were kind and forgiving pupils. Thank you for your trust and enthusiasm, and I look forward to continuing to contribute to the training of the next generations.

As we all know, the first steps of any professional journey begin long before a person reaches adulthood. I would like to thank my mother, Dr. Virginia Neal, for her support and encouragement throughout the years of a difficult upbringing and beyond. You have never let me believe I could fail. To my brothers, Richard, Thomas, and Michael, thank you for preparing me for a life in the trenches of law enforcement. Without your presence in my life, I would not know the value of family, loyalty, and the art of living genuinely and unafraid. For my late formative years, I want to thank my dear friend, Bette Schneider, for her insight, wisdom, and guidance. Her counsel and genius, through good times and bad, are directly responsible for the achievements of my life. I use lessons in life that you taught me every day, through the full range of my personal journey.

For the results of my years as a police officer, I would like to thank a number of my friends and colleagues from the Dallas Police Department. For Orville Stanton, who taught me that this profession was a worthwhile and bittersweet endeavor, not to be undertaken lightly. Forty years of age difference between us did not mean we could not speak the same language — the language of cops. To the instructors who kept me alive years after the academy was over — Dennis Mumford, Barbara Carey, Gary Croxdale, and

Hiram Burleson — you guys were "old school" and it made all the difference. For Rex Post, a second-to-none class advisor, I have never forgotten your personal insights into surviving "routine" patrol. Thank you for your passion and dedication to the field.

To all of my friends in DPD Class 249, especially the "Urban Warriors" Jerry Girdler, Israel Herrera, Scott Crump, Adolpho Perez, Ben Cintorino, Orlando Robinson, and Woody Leal, thank you for making the academy more fun for us all. You give a special meaning to the old song, "Bad Boys." I want to thank Sergeant Bruce Bryant, a supervisor with a heart of gold, for his support and advice through the years. For my field training officers from Northeast Patrol Division — Tom, Tim, and Barb — thank you for the memories, both good and bad. I learned the best of what I knew from you, in those early days. For my dear friends (you know who you are), who worked Channel 2 deep nights in the 1990s, I thank you for your words of wisdom in crucial moments, your collective sense of humor, and your dedication to making sure that we all went home safe, every morning. For all my brothers and sisters still on street patrol, stay safe and don't ever compromise your principles. You are the best of the best.

For Len Baxley, one of the most dedicated firearms trainers I ever met, my husband and I owe you a debt of gratitude which we can never repay. From you, I learned that all things happen for a reason. It is what we make of our life's circumstance that determines the true nature of our character.

From the Federal Air Marshals Service, there are a few highly dedicated people I would like to thank for their energy, tenacity, and inspiration. For the law enforcement trainers in Artesia, New Mexico, thank you for equipping us for a most dangerous mission: defending aircraft from terrorist attacks. For my classmates, especially Jeff, Red, Big John, and Alaska Rick, I enjoyed your camaraderie as we completed training together — on the sands, at the range, and beyond. From the Dallas field office, especially for Scott, Randy, Mike, Robert, Steve, Rex, Joe L., Joe G., Jet, and Kevin, your friendship and professionalism were second to none. May God continue to protect you in your most difficult assignments, whether domestically or abroad. Together, we have learned that some of our toughest battles are fought within ourselves. For all the other shooters: you are unseen, unheard, and unafraid in the chilly blue skies. I will never forget my time with you in the service of the citizens of the United States because you are the real heroes.

From the state of Maryland, I would like to give my sincere appreciation to the hard-working people of the Police and Correctional Training Commissions. For my good friends Rick and B.K., keep doing what you do best, saving student's lives one defensive tactics session at a time. I would like to thank Pat Bradley, a leader among men, and Lee Goldman, for his dedication to the field of police training for over forty years. You believed in my ability when others might have disregarded me. Also, for Dennis Murphey, you are a paragon of dignity and the definition of a straight shooter. I would follow your lead to the ends of the earth, anytime. I would like to thank Dr. Darla Rothman, for her tireless work in producing a manual for instructors that has served as "The Reference" for me over the past five years. For Helen Mashbaum, a long-suffering and congenial researcher par excellence, I thank you for providing a critical reading of my early work. Your suggestions were invaluable. For my mentor, Paul Hajek, I want to say that you never failed to hold me responsible for achieving my own success. Thank you for your vision of my potential; I owe you the greatest debt of all, for the gift of personal accountability.

Those with true wisdom realize that a person achieves nothing of value without the encouragement and commitment of their family. For my husband, Drew, a gifted emergency manager in his very nature, you are my personal superhero and the sum of all my dreams. There is only one person in the world with whom I want to share my life, whether good or bad, and that person is you. And, for my son, Andrew, you are the realization of all my hopes, just the way you are. May I endeavor to be worthy of your love and respect, throughout all of the years of your life.

—Ann

Author Biography

Ann Bumbak began her career in law enforcement in 1990 as a police/fire/ EMS dispatcher in Texas. After completing her undergraduate work, she joined the Dallas Police Department as a recruit. She rose to the rank of Senior Corporal while assigned to the Northeast Bureau, working in patrol as a field training officer. After the events of 9/11, she subsequently served as an undercover federal air marshal. Since leaving law enforcement field-work, she has been dedicated to improving police training programs, as a trainer, evaluator, and consultant in federal, state, and local law enforcement agencies. She has been privileged to work with a host of diverse agencies, including the Department of Homeland Security, State of Maryland, Federal Bureau of Investigation, and Drug Enforcement Administration, to design quality educational solutions for law enforcement.

The Current State of Police Training Programs

1

Start with the end in mind.

—**Stephen Covey**

The current state of formal police training programs is generally low quality and poorly administered. The issue is not the *intention* of the trainers, the vast majority of whom are passionate and dedicated professionals. The real dilemma is that competent, experienced police officers do not often make good educators because they have not been provided with the tools and training needed to become effective trainers.

An average police officer wears many hats in the course of his daily duties: social worker, therapist, urban soldier, surrogate parent, and role model. Police officers know how to command authority, manage criminal investigations, interact with the public, and discourse on topics from handguns to handlebars. When selected for training responsibilities, street officers bring a unique skill set to the academy setting — experience, enthusiasm about the profession, and knowledge of its potential pitfalls. Why then should these eager professionals fail when tasked with creating dynamic, classroom-based instruction?

Lack of effectiveness in the classroom is an almost certain outcome for the typical police trainer. Consider the case of Rob S., an experienced police officer who has been selected to work as a full-time trainer in the entry-level academy of a suburban police department. As a police officer with five years of experience, Rob is regarded as a successful professional by his peers and commanders. He is physically fit, intelligent, and interested in training others. After he is selected, he is sent to an unregulated, forty-hour course to gain certification as an instructor. He may have been instructed in adult learning principles, or perhaps not. He may or may not have an understanding of the role of educators, lesson plans, or facilitation in the classroom. Rob then reports for work an instructor and is tasked with teaching his first block of instruction on the history of law enforcement. He is handed a notebook of prepared material and told to acquaint himself with the topic by next week — the first week of a new police academy.

Rob has already been set up for failure as a police educator before he ever sets foot in the classroom. No matter what skills Rob may bring to his academy assignment — honed on the streets as a professional police officer and forged in battle over time with shift work, criminals, stress, and the other rigors of the job — he has not been given the basic tools for educating others. Can all of the essential knowledge and skills of a profession to which people devote years of their life in study, analysis, and reflection — teaching — be distilled into a forty-hour certification course? No. This is an impossible expectation, yet is the most common of circumstances in police departments around the country. We have failed in our mission to properly train law enforcement officers for a myriad of reasons.

The Historical Approach to Training

One of the contributing factors to lack of success in our ability to create and conduct training with exceptional results originates with the illustrious history of our profession and its traditional approach to managing training. Historically, police training has been informal and almost entirely on-the-job. With this approach, the field trainer must be both highly skilled *and* dedicated to the training goals of the department. The mindset of a trainer must be in harmony with the culture of his department or a difficult conflict emerges.

Though police trainers have a high level of commitment to improving the profession, keeping recruits alive, and passing on our essential knowledge, we are held hostage by the *mechanics* of the training process. Our hands have been veritably tied by bureaucratic processes that ensure each task (no matter how insignificant) is methodically checked off, thoroughly documented, and recorded. Trainer competence is nearly always a given. Commitment to training goals becomes increasingly difficult when department regulations clash with authentic street patrol functionality. In many cases, the essential tasks for the recruit officer in training are not tied to the reality of police work in any genuine way. The process of completing academy or field training has become a meaningless, form-intensive model, dissociated from the real needs of rookie police officers to learn *how to do the job*. It has become a method-focused exercise rather than a results-oriented mission.

Changing Demographics of Police Populations

Another issue central to the training dilemma is the changing demographics of police recruits and police trainers. The traditional recruit, as recently as the 1980s, was that of a blue-collar, working-class, white male with high school credentials. Likewise, many trainers in the field are still lacking in formal educational credentials with mixed results. Though trainers with college degrees can establish a dimension of credibility for police training programs, it is widely known that possession of both common sense and higher education is a rare instance.

However, recruiting departments now seek police officer candidates who are educated, articulate professionals from diverse backgrounds. Some departments even require that entry-level officers possess a baccalaureate degree. With higher education comes a host of issues that did not exist for our predecessors in law enforcement training. Recruits who enter the profession with college credentials respond well to the traditional adult education model, which is misunderstood and misapplied by well-intentioned police trainers. Expecting a collegiate atmosphere, these recruits are skeptical of attempts to engage their attention with off-the-cuff, unproven techniques. They recognize a cohesive program when they see it and are harsh critics of the inadequately designed materials used in many training academies. The result: a cynical attitude develops toward departmental training that skews an officer's perception of the department and the profession.

Knowing Our Limitations

Personal limitations of trainers themselves further compound the problem of adequate training. Many trainers have risen to their positions through proven competence in the field but have neglected their own educational needs along the way. The result: a strain in the ability to transmit important concepts, not due to lack of intrinsic ability but to lack of formal know-how. The old-fashioned, brutal approach to recruit training employed by the majority of trainers does not adequately address the expectations or needs of the more educated entry-level students of this generation.

Another roadblock to effective training is caused by the ever-expanding role of police officers in society. Whereas intervention in the family by law enforcement was formerly a rare event, police are now regularly coping with issues that were once the sole domain of parents. Police officers have full-time posts inside many public schools as school resource officers, where they serve as on-site protectors and mediators. The changing role of law enforcement in the public domain is just as significant. The availability of weapons, the proliferation of drugs and violent crimes, mandatory domestic violence enforcement mandates, and high-profile incidents contribute to more calls for police service. An increased concern about domestic terrorism has expanded police roles yet further. Police have more work to do than their allotted manpower can support.

Thus, the impetus for comprehensive entry-level police training is a profound responsibility. Criminal law, civil statutes, traffic codes, defensive tactics, officer survival, and countless other areas must be mastered. But there are simply too many conflicting priorities for training academies to do any topic true justice. Traditional mainstays of police work — interviewing, search-and-seizure laws, report writing and patrol operations — are marginalized in the academy, and classroom topics providing an overview of terrorism, incident command system, and cultural sensitivity bog down dynamic training opportunities with extended time in the classroom. Acquisition of raw knowledge is stressed over learning how to operate in the field. In one police training program in the Northeast, recruits were issued a 1,700-page criminal statute guide, as one of several mandatory textbooks. How much time was dedicated to the topic of criminal law in this program? *One week.*

A Downward Spiral

Because of their failure to understand and use the adult education model, police training programs are not structured to provide the level of excellence needed by contemporary law enforcement. Consequently, programs are not evaluated adequately and student retention of training is deeply affected. Consider the environment of the typical entry-level police training program. New officers are indoctrinated into the paramilitary culture over the course of weeks or months. They acquire a level of physical fitness, learn basic defensive tactics, and pass the obligatory police science courses. After graduation, rookies quickly acquaint themselves with the demands of street patrol. This training deficit continues once an officer is released to the field. Training, though important, is strictly limited once entry-level requirements have been met and often focuses on mandated, politically correct topics like anti-discrimination, defensive driving, and gang awareness. Once field training is complete, officers are sent for mandatory in-service training on rare occasions, often no more than eight hours per year.

What is in-service training like? Ask any police officer who has attended class in the past and he will tell you that it was boring, at best. There were probably a lot of "war stories" about the collectively funny or bizarre aspects of life as witnessed on the one side of the badge. If it was a highly technical class, there may have been a "death-by-slideshow" presentation. If the participants were very lucky, there might have been some collaterally related Internet videos showing assaults on police or resisting subjects being subjected to a dose of OC (pepper) spray or TASER®. The employment of multimedia materials is an afterthought rather than a mainstay of the training agenda; occasionally, the videos themselves *are* the showpiece of the presentation, with predictably poor results.

If we could continue to follow the career of an officer from new recruit to experienced officer, we would see how the training deficit continues to undermine the training program of a department as a whole. After a time in patrol, an officer may be promoted to corporal and selected as a field training officer. He may receive a one-week course to prepare him for this pivotal role. Instead of acquainting the new trainer with how to conduct the crucial on-the-job training that is dynamic and effective, the trainer is given an extensive course in how to complete written observation reports and how to recommend remedial training or termination and given the mantra, "Communication is important." There are limited opportunities to acquire the skills needed to directly train others *because there are no teachers who can model this skill* in the classroom environment. Training for trainers involves *hearing about* skills but not *active practice* of critical skills, like verbal counseling, remediation, and mentoring. This is a crucial mistake.

Finally, who delivers this all-important training to prepare officers to become trainers? Generally, other police officers, most of whom have no training in adult education principles. Some of these trainers have been assigned to the academy to solely serve the unending needs of the department. Certain officers may be assigned to classroom training roles because they are unable to work in the field because of a line-of-duty injury, traumatic experience, internal investigations, or politics. Other officers have been appointed to the training division for personal reasons. These officers may have an infant or ill spouse at home. They may have a short-term need for a day shift with weekends off, or they are simply unable to work in patrol or on other vigorous field assignments. It is only a slim minority of training officers who are genuinely interested in being in the classroom. It is not a matter of mindset — even trainers who are passionate about teaching are, too often, ineffective instructors. Why? The reason is this: because the organization has failed to develop their full potential. By providing them with too little access to the methods involved in dynamic program development, the organization has not invested in the trainers themselves. Even high-performing officers who seek assignment to the training division require solid, initial training to become effective instructors. It is an unfortunate truth that competence on the street is no measure of performance in the classroom.

The Challenges Ahead

Despite the great challenges facing police trainers, they are an affable and motivated group. Trainers work tirelessly to improve their programs, even without formal guidance or incentives. Many police trainers are interesting lecturers, captivating storytellers, and self-taught slideshow developers with a flair for the dramatic. Humor, too, abounds in the classrooms of the profession because law enforcement work is a strange yet delightful work environment, with outrageous features. Unfortunately, entertaining stories of personal experience are not always the most effective method for ensuring learning. Transmitting wisdom based on experience and conjecture is not the same as teaching. Trainers must be willing to take the risks associated with development to achieve the results they desire. The challenge is to achieve a synthesis by integrating their knowledge of the topic and awareness of their own teaching strengths with the best methods for transmission to the students. A comprehensive understanding of the gap between personal experience and student needs is the missing link in police training programs.

Law enforcement is an active, hands-on profession. People choose police work because they do not mind getting their hands dirty, figuratively speaking; in fact, they may actually like it. Sitting in a traditional classroom listening to an ordinary presentation does not routinely allow for hands-on action — the very foundation of law enforcement. Trainers who are not scholars of adult education program development find that they are woefully unprepared to achieve their full potential as police educators. By working "on the fly," as police officers are called on to do quite often in the field, trainers "wing" it in the classroom with existing lesson plans and it shows — in the chilly classroom reception and the training results.

The real message is clear: Educating police officers is often a doomed endeavor. The fact is that the vast majority of trainers have not internalized the principles embraced by adult educators in postsecondary environments. Specifically, the requirements for preparation, development, and understanding of the methodology in the adult learning model are summarily discarded for one of two approaches.

Approach #1: Entertain the students and cram the required material somewhere into your presentation.

Approach #2: Read (or have the students read aloud) the material from the book or slide presentation and ask whether everyone understands.

Trainers who are expected to design their own programs without significant understanding of accepted adult learning principles or leadership from an experienced adult educator are certain to fail. They are being tasked to do a job for which they have no intrinsic skill or training.

Yet, we cannot continue to blame the trainers for their inability. There is a systematic failure within our profession to prepare police training staff for the crucial tasks of program development and classroom delivery. Some critics may say that police trainers are not intellectually capable of understanding the goals of adult education due to a lack of educational credentials. Others will claim that the overriding contempt of formal education requirements in the pervasive police subculture subverts any attempts to educate its members. I disagree. Police officers can make great educators, regardless of their education (or lack thereof), age, gender, or experience level. Provided with a basic understanding of how adults learn and adequate tools for development, law enforcement trainers can become highly successful educators.

A Starting Point

How can we begin to refine our skills as police trainers? First, we must understand the mission at stake. A fundamental shift in mindset must occur when an officer becomes a dedicated trainer of police. Former field operations personnel who become full-time trainers of others require a significant education of their own before undertaking the task of instruction. Police organizations that send a new police instructor to a short course on instructional methods fall terribly short in preparing trainers to reach their full potential as educators. Furthermore, they are totally unprepared for development of new training modules to address emerging issues like active shooter, intelligence gathering, and forensic investigation methods. They are ill equipped, not in intellect, passion, or capability but merely in the ways and means to achieve dynamic training results. Put another way, they have the motivation but not the materials to get the job done — the "soul" but not the "science."

The overall approach to training in this profession requires a marriage of perspectives — that of a successful educator and street cop. In the coming chapters, we will explore the different aspects of the police training dilemma and the solutions to unlock success in the classroom. First, we will examine the history of training in the profession, with an emphasis on lessons learned from the field over the past thirty years. Next, we will discuss the challenges inherent in existing field training programs. Then, we will look more closely at the adult education model and curriculum development process adapted for the specific needs of law enforcement. We will explore strategies for maximizing potential in existing staff. An in-depth analysis of the use of scenario-based learning will follow, incorporating examples of successful integration of classroom-based instruction and practical application of "hands-on" skills. Finally, we will emphasize the importance of adequate training programs from a liability perspective.

Developing active, dynamic training for police professionals is a crucial need. Without well-designed training programs, police officers cannot perform the most difficult tasks demanded by modern society — peacekeeping, enforcement of laws, and protection of those in need. If we fail to train police officers effectively, the consequences are exceedingly harsh. Lives of recruits, officers, and civilians are at stake and we must not continue to fail in the task set before us. With the advent of increasing liability and litigation, training adequately and successfully is a timely concern for departments around the country. As police trainers, we must hold ourselves to a higher standard of competence as educators before we can effectively train others.

Historical Perspectives on Police Training

2

... We were a block farther along when I heard a high-speed "pssst" sound as a bullet flew past my ear. By the time I whirled around to shoot back, I saw only a flash of a figure retreating and ducking around the corner. Though my finger was pressed on the trigger, I never fired. What was I supposed to do? Miss and take out a little kid and his mother?

—**Robert Cole**

In his fascinating book, *Under the Gun in Iraq*, Cole described the challenges of working as a field training officer in post-occupation Iraq. Venturing beyond the classroom, he denoted the marked differences in culture, mindset, and history of the region as exceptionally difficult to overcome. Tasked with training Iraqi police officers in the full range of duties, from patrol to community policing, he explained the perspective required when police officers operate in a war zone: tact, self-control, and prudent decision-making abilities under extreme stress.

Many field trainers in the United States now find themselves facing some of the same circumstances as Cole. Faced with training new generations who value different concepts of what is appropriate and effective in policing, the culture of younger recruits presents a veritable challenge to train differently. This dissention in ideology is merely a symptom of larger changes in society at large, and police training programs are not the only casualties to suffer.

Training Soldiers and Police: Parallels and Contrasts

As perceptions change over time within society, preferences mutate and evolve. As recently as 1960, for example, a glaring and serious Uncle Sam pointed directly to the reader and pronounced "I want you — for the U.S. Army." Viewers of this slogan must have responded to the idea of belonging to a group, working as a team, and the intrinsic purpose of personal sacrifice as important for the country. They volunteered in droves to enlist and manage two twentieth-century wars.

By 2001, the situation had changed. Recruiters were no longer able to make their recruiting goals, for various and debatable reasons. The slogan was changed. "Be All That You Can Be," with a catchy sing-song, was soon followed by an even more individual appeal. "I Am ... an Army of One" pronounced the lone soldier traipsing across mountains, fields, and streams, wearing full camouflage, in primetime television commercials. The message: you can be a highly trained, thoroughly awesome soldier on your own — just sign up and fulfill your own personal destiny.

Comparing the Uncle Sam with the Army of One slogan, it is clear that, in our society, the concept has become less about team effort and more about individual achievement. This clever alteration in marketing strategy by the military was quite successful and underscores a keen understanding of the changing attitudes of society. Like the military, police training programs must undertake the difficult task of responding to the increasing expectations of society. Unfortunately, these changing expectations make police training more difficult than ever to both develop and manage well.

As trainers know, there are many parallels between military and police service. We are both uniformed professions, governed by a strict chain of command, fiercely self-reliant, and ultimately proud of our methods and means. Thus, what is the difference between training combat soldiers and the "urban soldiers" of police work? Put simply, as Robert Cole learned in Iraq, the rules of engagement. Police recruits in our times must learn that they cannot act with blanket impunity against the enemy, because the enemy combatants are not always readily apparent. Our "customers," the criminal element, blend in well with normal members of society and, generally, violence committed by police officers is frowned upon by civilians.

The difference between soldiers and police is highly apparent, operationally speaking. Whereas soldiers can be trained to fire on the enemy without prejudice, police cannot. Officers must be fully trained to identify potential enemies, operate independently without a command structure, and, when force is required, use only that amount of force that is reasonable and necessary to stop the threat. Imagine if Special Forces units were tasked with using only "reasonable force" in wartime operations, while rescuing hostages or conducting counterterrorist missions. Potential atrocities committed in wartime are left for posterity to determine in hindsight, whereas split-second use-of-force errors made in law enforcement are published complete with an expert analysis and indictment on the nightly news.

The Traditional Approach

To genuinely understand the mythic struggle within the profession to legitimize police education programs, one must be acquainted with the history of law enforcement training. For much of the preceding century, the newly sworn officer completed a short course in law and order and was handed over to an experienced field training officer (FTO). The FTO was the final authority on training, with little, if any, fixed period for on-the-job instruction.

Not only was the FTO a mentor, supervisor, and partner, he was the person responsible for indoctrination of the recruit into the police subculture. One colleague described this experience as a lingering farewell to adolescence through discovery of a "more legal" outlet for the assorted follies of youthfulness:

> … Instead of racing cars and raising hell on the wrong side of the law, I joined the force and did it on the job with my buddies, who were cops. In what other profession could I get paid to chase bad guys, impress women and carry a gun?

This officer, destined for the ranks of command twenty years later, summarized the initial years of his police experience as among the best of his life. Yet, times have changed. And, some say, it is not for the better for police officers.

The Role of the Media

Perceptions of police have changed markedly over the past century; one of the most significant contributing reasons for this change is the widespread influence of television. The proliferation of police-oriented dramas in prime-time television has fueled the public's fascination with the so-called thin blue line. Police-themed dramas, whether realistic or not, dictate the average citizen's perception of the role of police officers. More sinister, the deliberate attempt in some quarters to paint police as bigoted bullies, self-aggrandizing and arrogant in their approach to street work, creates a tenuous and volatile workplace, especially in urban areas. High-profile, media-driven incidents of reported police brutality, like that of the Rodney King incident in 1991, contribute to creating even more difficult training and operating conditions.

It is important for police trainers to understand that the media both reacts and contributes to the changing spectrum of society's perceptions of law enforcement. Some aspects of the police profession have become more in vogue in recent years — for example, crime scene investigation (or commonly CSI) — through media exposure. As any experienced officer knows, crime scene forensics work is anything but glamorous. The vast majority of police departments do not have the resources to hire dedicated crime scene personnel; this duty becomes yet another unsettling task for the new patrol officer. The reality of the job — sifting through the bullet fragments, bodily fluids, and other human detritus — certainly humbles even the most television-saturated, starry-eyed rookie officer.

Additionally, courtesy of the media influence, a more significant change has occurred in the stereotype of the police over the past fifty years. Whereas once the bumbling "Officer Friendly" was the norm, the darker image of the abusive, controlling cop has now emerged. The transformation from a fictional figure that is less the harmless Barney Fife and more the harrowing Detective Sipowicz is a significant commentary on society's contemporary opinion of the police.

Evolving Approaches to Police Training

Like media-created images, vocations also evolve over time. There has been a subtle shift over the last thirty years within the profession to reinvent police work as a vocation characterized by high standards and a new national identity. This identity emphasizes a professional code of ethics, ongoing education requirements, and a formal licensure process. This is not to say that police ever aspired to be anything *less* than ethical or professional. It is merely a movement to reclassify it with a more prestigious moniker, or handle. Like the professions of nurse, attorney, and engineer, the traditional on-the-job skills acquisition approach has been refined to include stringent entry requirements, formalized training programs, and mandatory continuing education.

How has the shift within law enforcement affected training programs? The effort to remake law enforcement as a white-collar profession has been only partially successful for three reasons. First, for many years, the on-the-job training (OJT) that was conducted for police officers was the standard in the industry. The reason is simple: OJT worked. Officers instinctively knew that academy training was just the beginning of the requisite police education — just as they do today. The streets of any police district, small or large, provided the best training environment of all. Coping with real calls for service, actual citizens, and just doing the job day to day filled the void between the academy training and the reality of police work. OJT, though generally viewed with contempt by commentators from polite society as the old-fashioned approach, embodied all of the essential elements of police work. In these "good, old days," officers who performed poorly on field training were not retained, based solely on the advice of the field training officer. No documentation or defense of this decision was required. The spectral threat of litigation based on harassment or discrimination was not yet a reality in the United States. As a result, trainers could call it like they saw it, especially with regard to hiring and retention practices.

Second, with an increasing awareness of the need for objectivity in hiring and retention practices, the training paradigm for law enforcement evolved into something new. Where there had once been an informal process of assess and instruct, observe and correct, a formal process emerged with guidelines, rules, and examinations. The critical and honest opinions of the training officer were replaced by set-in-stone, bureaucratic procedures, cumbersome checklists, and rigid rules governing all aspects of academy training and OJT. Academies were lengthened into longer stays — up to eight months, in some programs — in an attempt to train on every possible topic. Once a recruit graduated, he still went through an OJT process. However, the field training officer's personal input was singularly removed from the process of evaluation — they were tasked with becoming all "bark" and no "bite." FTOs were programmed to complete adequate written documentation alone, regardless of actual training needs or deficiencies. In the pursuit of these uniform results, a crucial element has been lost: recruit job competence. As a result, training quality has suffered crucial setbacks in the name of progress, equality, and uniformity.

The Challenge of Diversity

Diversity concerns present a host of challenges for the uninitiated field training officer. Training recruits through stereotypical hazing, embarrass-ment, and other inappropriate means have long ceased to be useful; most trainers would agree that old-fashioned methods are just not up to the task. However, modern police trainers need an approach that does not rely on a one-size-fits-all method. Though diversity has made our profession an infi-nitely better one, it is now a more complicated job in which to train others. This is not to say that diversity in the ranks is unimportant; in fact, diversity is critical to the law enforcement missions to protect and serve all citizens. Especially in areas with high crime and low income, it is absolutely essential to have police representatives of every color, background, and gender avail-able to intervene with the resident populations.

Women officers are routinely called upon to interview children and female victims of sexual assault not because their male counterparts are not able to do so but because the female officers are perceived as more effective with those victims.* Likewise, victims of color report more comfort with officers of their own race because of the ethnic officer's perceived sensitiv-ity to racial and cultural mores and traditions. Unquestionably, professional police officers of any color can be significant role models to the youth in the underprivileged areas they serve. A veteran corporal, an African American officer with twenty years' experience, once summed up his understanding of race-based policing in this way:

You are out here trying to help *your* people. I am out here trying to help *mine* ...

---

* Some studies have indicated that this is not, in fact, a true statement. Surprisingly, women police officers have been shown to act less compassionately to victims of rape and other sex crimes, for reasons that are under continual debate. However, the percep-tion that women police are better at coping with this kind of call still endures.

Training female officers has further complicated the role of the FTO. Traditionally a very male-dominated profession, women are increasingly entering the ranks of the uniformed police services. Some experienced officers question how female officers can adequately support the mission of the police department, when fitness standards are altered to suit female upper body strength limitations and cardiovascular endurance. A surprising statistic is the lack of assaults and injuries sustained by women police officers in the line of duty. This finding is not debunked by the myth that women officers do not take enforcement action as often as their male counterparts. The conclusion is clear: female officers can be just as effective as male officers, although they may be more challenging to field train.

The Educated Recruit

The changing face of law enforcement also brings other challenges. Most commonly, police trainers report universally increasing levels of frustration with police recruits who are college educated. These recruits — often characterized as overeducated and arrogant — present a stereotypical rejection of the FTO's knowledge, based on years of experience on the street. Though they clearly seek a distillation of the FTO's understanding, especially with regard to survival and effectiveness, they reject the manifold, age-old methods used to keep order and manage society. New officers who were raised in the now-popular parenting style of indulgence and individuation find themselves alienated by the police culture that places badge carriers as a group ahead of the single officer. Within the profession, we refer to this issue as *generational strain*. The experienced officer struggles with the need to communicate key concepts to the rookie officer who enters the profession with higher education and a more pronounced opinion of the proper role of the police. Meanwhile, the rookie officer looks with disdain on the aging FTO role model who attempts to indoctrinate him into the way things are done out on the street.

Rookie officers have often described their field training experience with an emphasis on the personality of the FTO as critical to the success or failure of any given recruit. Like recruits, FTOs can develop a reputation that is quite different from their own personality. For some recruits, this can spell training disaster for a term of weeks or months that they are under supervision.

One college-educated officer described his FTO experience this way:

> I couldn't do anything right. I would try to do what he said, and he would criticize me anyway. I couldn't drive, I couldn't write reports, and I couldn't talk to people without getting corrected. ...

Clearly, little regard was accorded to the recruit officer-in-training about how he preferred to be treated. In some cases, recruits are removed from their assigned FTOs because of personality clashes, refusal to train, or failure to follow orders. In general, however, recruits are expected to cope with the training officer or face serious consequences.

Surviving Field Training

There is universal agreement on one aspect of field training: developing new recruits is a difficult task. Recruits new to the field are evaluated based on their academy reputation (however sparse), responsiveness, attitude, and performance. FTOs generally loathe judging a book by its cover but are quickly able to note when an officer's appearance is likely to cause a problem on the streets. Officers who are small, meek, or significantly overweight are at a disadvantage from the first day on the job. However, it has become not politically correct to comment on a recruit officer's appearance, even when this creates a safety issue. Likewise, in a short time, the frantic, inappropriate, and lazy are easily identified by the experienced trainer. Transcending the obvious categories, however, the officers who truly cannot do the job often do not stay for long, succumbing to injuries, peer rejection, or disciplinary reasons.

There have been several mainstream approaches to the management of field training over the past fifty years. One approach, the San Jose model, delegates field training to three different trainers who guide the recruit through activities of increasing autonomy over four separate phases, encompassing a period of twenty or more weeks. Following rigorous academy training, the recruit reports for duty to his station, where he meets his initial FTO, who trains him for Phase I and evaluates him when he returns for Phase IV. This beginning and end approach allows one experienced trainer to see the final result of the recruit's OJT training from day one in the field.

Phase I introduces the recruit to field operations. In the initial days, the recruit observes and shadows the FTO as the FTO responds to calls and makes traffic stops. After the shadowing period is complete, the recruit begins basic police tasks under the careful direction of the FTO — driving the patrol vehicle, communicating via radio, and filling out forms like traffic citations and booking forms. By the end of Phase I, the goal ratio of work for the recruit is about 25 percent; thus, 75 percent of the patrol work is still being done by the FTO. In Phase II, the recruit moves toward a more equal relationship of workload with the FTO; the aim is to be capable of 50 percent of the work by the end of the phase. Phase III marks the beginning of independence for the recruit, who consults with the FTO for assistance when needed but is expected to demonstrate his capabilities as a self-sufficient officer in the near future. Phase IV is observation-only status for the FTO as the recruit returns to his initial trainer for a final evaluation. During Phase IV, the recruit officer must be capable of managing full duty (or 100 percent) of the patrol activity to be released from the field training program.

Remedial training for new officers is a reality of the police field training process. Training gaps exist, in that academy settings can only be realistic to a small degree when compared with the streets. As one trainer cynically wrote:

> Realistic training involving use of deadly force is generally frowned upon by administrators. Thus, we use the FATS [shooting simulation] machine instead of live fire exercises to test a recruit's judgment.

A range of other problems is commonly noted. Recruits who cannot read or write adequately cannot prepare professional reports. Inability to communicate well verbally with the trainer or, even worse, with citizens creates a significant difficulty in the field. As previously mentioned, physical limitations can be problematic, especially in high-crime areas where rigorous and dangerous police foot pursuits may occur.

I suggest that all areas of deficiency in field training are surmountable obstacles; given enough time, every area of remediation can be accomplished successfully. There is one exception: the development of bearing. In my experience, the majority of the difficulty in field training lies in the development of the appropriate bearing for police officers. Without proper bearing, the developing recruit has no compass for his behavior with citizens. Many recruits enter police service without the benefit of a military background. Without this preparation, they enter police work with the mindset of a civilian, heart and soul. As a result, they are more likely to identify with victims and suspects. This tendency to identify with civilians can lead to a dangerous situation: lack of situational awareness.

A recruit must learn to master the inherent dichotomy of law enforcement: at any scene, you are either in *charge* or in *trouble*. Although a recruit may be a caring and concerned person underneath, he is vested with the authority to take away a person's freedom or, indeed, his life. The civilians, whether law-abiding or criminal, never forget this fact; it governs all interactions they have with police officers.

Some recruits cannot develop the necessary bearing to do the job. As field trainers, we have a vital imperative to fulfill: our trainees must be able to survive their career in police work. Recruits who cannot write a good report are at risk for losing a case in criminal court or having a citation dismissed. Recruits who cannot become officers of appropriate bearing risk more than any other type of recruit. Without an understanding of the risks of the job, they cannot see the danger they will face as the theoretical sheep in wolf's clothing. They must be removed from the profession — not because they cannot physically do the job but because the job will cost them their life. It is the field trainer's highest imperative to identify these recruits and help them gracefully exit from police work.

Conclusion

If police trainers are the gatekeepers of the law enforcement profession, field trainers are the absolute final authority on preparedness for entry into unsupervised police work. If we disregard the input of field trainers, we have no valid training program. Training police officers is an inherently difficult task. Media images distort the reality of police work in a way that further complicates our role as trainers. Barring a background in military service, recruits enter law enforcement with the mindset of a civilian. Without proper bearing, a recruit cannot be retained because of the likelihood that he or she may become a casualty. As the final authority, field trainers must be decisive, firm individuals when determining when a recruit is ready for release from supervision.

However, field trainers merely inherit the product that the academy trainers have turned out. To begin to affect the performance of our street-level forces, we must undertake a thorough examination about what is done well (and poorly) before a recruit reaches FTO training. Let's undertake a retrospective of training — examining the process from the beginning and the inside out — to more effectively understand where dynamic police training begins.

Four Steps to Initiating Change in Instructional Programs

3

> He is the true enchanter, whose spell operates not on the senses, but on the imagination and heart.
>
> —**Washington Irving**

The true success of any organization rests in the capability of its educators. Without competent trainers, police education does not succeed in its most basic function — preparing entry-level law enforcement officers for patrol duties. The quality of the training given is in direct correlation with the engagement, enthusiasm, and professional development of the staff members who give it. Positive, energetic instructors create dynamic training opportunities by their very nature, and it is these opportunities that produce the solid results of student performance. Consequently, no results can be achieved without a substantial investment in individual trainers to maximize their full potential.

Truly, the failure to implement a well-designed trainer development program foretells a slow decline in training results. Yet, in times of budget crises, training is often one of the first priorities to be cut. This penny-wise, pound-foolish approach by administrators is in fundamental opposition to the obvious reality of predictable and diminishing returns.

Yet, how important is training? Let's examine this example. In one mid-sized police department in the Midwest, *no training of any kind* was provided for newly promoted criminal investigators. These investigators transitioned from uniformed police corporals and field trainers to newly minted detectives overnight. The predictable result: an extremely steep, almost insurmountable learning curve. Tasked with investigation, interview, and interrogation of suspects for offenses ranging from kidnapping to bank robbery with no training, cases were notoriously difficult to properly document and prepare for prosecution, resulting in many court-ordered dismissals. When questioned about the lack of training provided to these detectives, the police executive reported that the department could not afford the training classes, both in terms of lost manpower hours and a cost of approximately $300 per detective. Unfortunately, the substantial cost to society in terms of cases lost or dismissed and criminals not prosecuted due to lack of training is incalculable.

Without adequate training and mentors, police officers cannot succeed in their crucial duty to society. When organizational support is withheld or withdrawn from the maintenance of good programs and new program development is shelved in the hopes for better fiscal times, police educators are ill equipped to manage the resulting fallout. Police recruits become likened unto cattle — "Get 'em in and move 'em out." Training to the minimum standards becomes the end goal. The unfortunate results of this kind of mentality will not be seen until the recruits graduate to the streets, perhaps not for years. Yet, under the pressures of performance required by society, poorly trained police officers will devolve into the icons of hostility, brutality, and incompetence so popularized in the liberal media.

Accepting the responsibility to train others is among the most noble of professional callings. Police trainers who answer the call to provide the next generation with the skills needed to survive police work deserve recognition for their sacrifice and dedication. As a profession, we must learn to invest more in the people involved in the process and invest less in the process itself. Instead of handing trainers the curriculum binders and telling them to simply go forth and train, we must give the trainers the tools and tricks for designing the curriculum so they may go forth and develop. In doing so, we allow them to become stewards of the programs they design, instead of simply caretakers of broken, existing programs.

The consequence of the failure to invest in trainers is significant. Over time, given attrition, retirement, and chronic lack of support, the most highly qualified trainers will not remain long in training assignments. Supervisors of training staff have a tremendous burden in that they must attract and retain skilled educators — an impossible task when the training environment is not conducive to self-improvement. Thus, to invest in students, we must first invest in the instructors. The instructors must then develop and maintain excellence in the programs they create. How is this achieved? Let's take a closer look at a solution.

Skinning the Cat

It has been said that there are many ways to skin a cat. This means that we have many, many options as to how we will achieve any mission. We can use traditional tools and methods, or we can formulate a new approach. Translated for our purposes as trainers, this phrase means that we need to empower instructors to be creative in the ways and means of achieving training goals.

Let's examine this principle in action. You, the trainer, determine that there is a need for a block of instruction on the use of verbal commands. The objective of your course is to introduce students to the use of an authoritative, command voice. Using your knowledge of the topic, you determine that you would like for all students to have an opportunity to practice this skill before the class ends. How will you "skin the cat" for this class? What approach will you use to meet your mission objectives? Let's explore three options.

Choice A: You Will Tell Them

"I will tell you..."

FOCUS: Instructor

Choice A is the traditional, lecture-oriented approach. With this method, you will talk at length about the importance of using a clear, authoritative voice, tell some "war stories" about your experiences, and then perhaps demonstrate the command voice for the class. The advantages of Choice A are that you need very little preparation to teach this topic, no materials, and a minimal (or no) lesson plan. However, with Choice A, there is little or no opportunity for student practice and, thus, a passive (and generally, bored) audience. This is the most common method of training in the law enforcement profession.

Choice B: Some Will Tell You

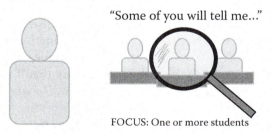

"Some of you will tell me..."

FOCUS: One or more students

Choice B is the alternative, middle-of-the-road approach. You will ask the students to tell you the difference between a command voice and a weak voice, drawing out the important points from the statements of the students themselves. Then, you will have students volunteer to demonstrate the "right" and "wrong" ways. The advantage of Choice B is that the students will control the learning. With Choice B, some students have an opportunity to practice, whereas others do not. This choice is a major improvement over the traditional model but still lacks a key element.

Choice C: All Will Show and Tell You

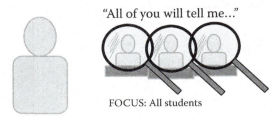

"All of you will tell me..."

FOCUS: All students

Choice C is yet another option, the learner-centered approach. In this approach, you will lead a discussion about the need for the command voice. Next, you will invite the participation of every student by designing an exercise in which students will be exposed to a series of mock incidents requiring the use of a command voice. This is the basic tenet of scenario-based training. Students will then participate in evaluating the success or failure of their peers with your role as the *facilitator* only. Following this exercise, you will sum up the key points.

Choice C allows you to be the captain of the course but allows the students to drive the learning process. With this choice, all students can participate to the degree that they wish to contribute. However, Choice C is highly labor intensive, requiring the maximum amount of preparation, writing, and careful execution. Is all of this effort worthwhile? Absolutely, because when you gain 100 percent participation and engagement, learning occurs within multiple domains — mental, physical, and emotional. Students who feel a connection with the material through hearing it, seeing it, working with it, and developing a personal opinion about their experience will retain and use the information that has been delivered.

Skinning the cat is the planning stage of training, where the decisions are made about how to conduct a training session. There are literally hundreds of approaches to training others, using any number of methods and materials. Given any topic, an instructor has an unlimited number of possibilities for how he or she will accomplish the objectives. Ensure that if the goals are set in stone, the methods to train to those goals are not. How an instructor will skin the cat should be his decision and within his control.

I suggest that to achieve the maximum results in training, we must distance ourselves from the "old way" of doing things. The old way demands that we continue in the steps of our predecessors, who designed and delivered the same program in the same way, year after year. This approach eliminates the absolutely human factor involved in the process of training others effectively. Where one teacher may prefer a rhetorical argument, another may gravitate toward concrete discussions or class debate on hard facts. Some instructors favor the dramatic approach of skits or role-play; others are mortified by the mere idea of such activities and prefer to train in a more sober, straightforward way.

Whatever the instructor's personal disposition, dynamic training results can be achieved in the classroom and beyond through a definable process. This process begins with the understanding that instructors must be given complete dominion over the presentation methods. Thus, we must become *results* driven, not *process* driven.

Stop Lecturing

Any instructor who proclaims that lecture is the only way that a topic can be taught is a poor student of adult education principles. Lecture is an ineffective technique because the vast majority of adults do not want to be lectured, not even by a subject matter expert. The small minority of people who do enjoy a good lecture are very rare people indeed in law enforcement. In fact, in a state study conducted in the Northeast, less than 5 percent of the police in-service populations assessed over a period of several years reported that they preferred lecture-based instruction. Why? The answer: law enforcement students are not inherently passive and reflective people. The personality profile of an average police officer is often described by psychological researchers as action oriented, impulsive, and decisive. Do individuals with these traits like to sit passively in a classroom and receive verbal direction from others about concepts, ideas, or activities? No. Therefore, we must stop lecturing in our police classrooms.

The options open to the instructor who rejects lecture-based instruction are as diverse as the imagination. The beginning of really divergent training is in the careful selection of the methods used to gain and keep the student's interest and "buy-in" to the material. An instructor can develop or deter the audience's interest in the first sixty seconds of any training session. Make those crucial first moments the best material you can create. In addition to delivering quality materials, trainers must develop a persona that can educate as well as entertain. For law enforcement, this can mean a judicious use of lecture (no longer than two to three minutes at any one time), punctuated by question-and-answer, structured activities, and hands-on practice. Action-oriented audiences want to be involved in working with a topic, not just hearing about it.

Become intimately acquainted with the subject material before determining how you will present it in the classroom. Too often, minimal time is invested in preparing to train. Instructors rely on their memory of high school or college classes — the epitome of lecture-based instructional models. Given no other direction, trainers have no choice but to execute instruction on the basis of very limited skills in public speaking. Educate yourself about dynamic presentation methods and use those skills to teach others in your units, departments, and organizations.

An Accurate Mirror

Dedication to self-improvement as an instructor first requires a diligent study of effective instructors and the science behind their classroom techniques. The secondary process of continuing to self-educate, through reading, writing, and attending instructor development courses, must be ongoing. This book is one source of information about this process, but there are many other sources of inspiration. President Abraham Lincoln once said that if he were given eight hours to cut down a tree, he would spend six hours sharpening his ax. The same principle applies to the refinement of training skills. Without finely honed skills, even the most engaging trainers will fail to achieve the results they want.

Cultivating true excellence as a trainer requires a personal commitment to discovery of your areas of strength and weakness and the fortitude to examine true measures of your own performance. These measures of performance are not as simple as student test scores or the typical "smile sheets" of instructor evaluations. We must challenge ourselves to look deeper at the fundamental nature of training we provide and the end results on the students' behaviors, attitudes, and knowledge and thus the impact on the organization as a whole. We must begin to realize that a complex process emerges when a trainer undertakes the role of effective police educator: plan, teach, reflect, and evaluate.

The great educator Stephen Covey suggested that in order to achieve maximum results and life-changing internal experiences, a person must endeavor to live outside of his personal "script" and begin to live out of his "imagination" instead. The script is the sum total of the daily training routine and the past experiences that have shaped our own image of ourselves as instructors. In contrast, the imagination is the perception and understanding of the instructors we would like to become. Applying this concept to police training means this: An instructor can free himself from the confines of the preprogrammed educational experience that has been scripted for him in the past. In other words, just because "it has always been done this way" does not mean it cannot be changed for the better. Existing training programs that are fatally flawed and egregiously wrong by their very design can be overcome, given enough time devoted to the development and careful cultivation of desire and motivation of the instructor.

In order to begin this process, police trainers must take a hard look in the mirror to ascertain their reasons for being in the academy. Many trainers relish the absolute, unchallenged power they derive from being vested with the title of drill instructor or class advisor to recruits. As a result, they live out those scripted relationships with students based on their own experiences of past degradation or humiliation. Are you, the trainer, seeking the validation, recognition, or simple brutish authority derived from exerting power over others? If you find that you are acting out of this kind of script, you must examine your conscience and determine whether you are prepared to put aside your personal baggage and/or soapbox to become a better trainer. If you cannot or will not do so, you have no place in training others.

After ascertaining your reasons for wanting to train others, devote some time to uncovering the true picture of what kind of trainer you want to become. Do you want to be the hard, emotionally distant yet encouraging leader? Do you picture yourself as an upright role model of fitness and tact or a caring, approachable mentor? Examine your personal life story for examples of honorable, motivating people to follow. There are also inspirational role models to be discovered in the annals of history, literature, and even contemporary news. From these examples, draw inspiration to better yourself as an educator and person of principle.

Over the years, other professional trainers have shared their choices of personal heroes with me. One friend epitomized General Colin Powell as the most earnest example of an uncompromising leader. Another characterized his late father, who was shamefully persecuted as a minority in the Deepest South, as his paragon of positive attitude under fire, fierceness, and grace. Another fellow trainer admitted that his hero was the great actor John Wayne, because he was forever the tough, rugged lawman who settled disputes with swiftness, a gun, and his irascible wit. Almost every trainer has had an experience with at least one genuine leader in the past. Living out of the imagination challenges trainers to internalize that leader's qualities and begin to project those qualities in the classroom. Do not underestimate the power of personal heroes in your quest for self-improvement; instinctively rely on those images that internally awaken your sense of awe and respect.

Trusting in Trainer Ingenuity

Essentially, cultivating excellence in instructors can be distilled into a two-fold process. First, organizations must support high-quality train-the-trainer (T4T) programs to equip police instructors with the skills they need to become true educators and not simply lecturers. Without ongoing training to keep their skills sharp, instructors become stale and static in their roles. Instructors should return to the lowly status of student for at least one class per year to refine their skills. Whether it is a new credential in fitness training, defensive tactics, firearms, slide presentation development, or other topic, trainers need to be reminded what it is like to be the scholars, and not the masters, of the system.

Second, once the T4T supports are in place, agencies must learn to trust their instructors with developing their own solutions to existing training dilemmas. Executive leadership may ask: How will instructors solve problems effectively without direction from management? Let's examine a recent example of an instructor-generated solution. An academy in the Southeast lacked all the equipment needed for implementing a scenario-based learning (SBL) program; they had no furniture or props of any kind to deploy this pivotal change in training. Leadership executives declared that, despite their support for the move to SBL, the needed funds would not become available for years. However, a key instructor of the program was determined not be stymied by the lack of resources. As a result, he collected furniture and props from garage sales and the local dump; he solicited local barrooms to donate posters, empty beer cans, and liquor bottles for the program to add to the realism of scenarios.

Through one man's tireless dedication to see this project through to fruition, he inspired the incumbent academy students and teachers to assist him in his quest for free or nearly free items. Recruits and instructors donated items in droves; most remarkably, the class designed and built an L-shaped wooden bar for a mock tavern, using their own skills, tools, and materials. The class presented the academy with this remarkable item three weeks before graduation, affixed with a small bronze plaque bearing their class number and motto. The pride evident in the construction and endowment of the wooden bar was apparent. The end result was the complete outfitting of five SBL rooms, including a tavern, convenience store, bedroom, living room, and hotel room within six months. Total net cost to the police academy: zero dollars.

Trainers need to be invested with the ability to decide how they will implement training goals and meet the course objectives. Police officers are shrewd, creative, and insuperable individuals. As police trainers, we are intrinsically endowed with the knowledge to overcome obstacles to effective training. Once forged in the furnace of street patrol, police officers never forget the remarkable journey from the academy hall to urban sprawl. Experienced officers who become police trainers recognize the training gaps in classroom materials. Ask for their input. Managers must learn to trust their staff with the ways and means of solving these problems.

In any case, police trainers must be empowered to decide the instructional method (the "how"), even if they do not decide the instructional content (the "what") of a course. In jurisdictions where curriculum is developed by committee or mandated materials must be used, the trainers must still have input into how they will achieve the course goals using those materials. Without full stewardship of the materials used to instruct, all but the top tier of trainers will be much less effective.

A Training Experiment

An initial experiment into this process is simple to conduct. Revise the materials you already have in place. Trainers should first work to master adult education principles of learner-centered instructional methodology and then apply them to the existing training curriculum. Select the most boring, lecture-based course in the academy repertoire and revise it to include group activities, hands-on practice, and student debate or discussion using the principles in this book. Allow no more than three minutes of lecture at any given time. Challenge trainers to develop activity-based learning for the class. Can this even be done for a traditionally boring topic like report writing or use of force? Yes. And I will prove it, using the chapters of this book.

Once staff trainers have mastered revising the lecture-based curriculum, they should select a single topic of personal expertise to develop new curricula. Instructors with a high level of interest in topics like officer survival, accident reconstruction, interviewing sexual assault victims, and the like can now bring those skills into play as trainers. Work as a training team or committee to develop objectives, if needed. Aim for higher levels of student comprehension through an emphasis on active learning and student practice. Consider the cognitive, affective, and psychomotor perspectives. Ensure that the objectives are measurable. Set down these concepts on paper and execute around the objectives using the principles in this book. Use an accepted lesson plan format and take the time to do it well. The results will speak volumes.

Every journey of self-improvement has the potential for painful growth. As such, every training program requires a conscientious, periodic evaluation of the instructors to ascertain the results. Police training program managers should solicit the input of experienced educators about the teaching ability of the academy instructors. Request an unbiased opinion from a professional educator who is a true stranger to the subject being developed. I suggest an English, psychology, or history professor, ideally from a local university or community college; these fields of study require above-average communications skills and this will work to your advantage as an administrator. Have the guest sit in on the class and offer written comments about the instructor's presentation skills, materials, lesson plans, and teaching ability in an unstructured way. Ask for an honest appraisal and constructive advice in the form of open note-taking, not formal evaluation forms. After all, we should remember that police instructors are generally police officers first and educators second. Do not hesitate to ask for proactive input from trained adult educators, who will be honored to assist local law enforcement training endeavors.

Conclusion

In conclusion, the most important aspect of any police training program is the trainers themselves, the essential human element. Without adequate investment in time and resources from administrators, police trainers

Addressing Adult Learning Styles

4

I hear and I forget. I see, I remember. I do, I understand.

—Confucius

The quickest route to taking existing instruction from the mediocre to the memorable is through the development of an understanding of adult learning preferences. Yet, a fundamental lack of knowledge about basic learning styles is pervasive in the police training culture. Why? For many years, trainers have focused on "teaching to the test" to ensure compliance with mandated scoring goals. Rote memorization, employing clever acronyms, and a tendency to test and then forget crucial material have been used as common practices in police academies nationwide for years. The result of these methods is equivocal: students may pass objective-based tests adequately but have no in-depth comprehension of the topics covered. The final product is a police recruit or operating professional who cannot apply the lessons learned to real-life situations — the defining principle of police work.

As previously discussed in Chapter 3, I suggest that a strict emphasis on lecture-based instruction leads to a classroom environment that is universally despised by police officers in training. Attempts to supplement lectures with an amateurish slide presentation further exacerbate the learning void. Many a law enforcement professional has been subjected to hours (or even weeks) of instruction, facilitated by a poor presenter reading slides to the audience, caught up in his or her own internal perceptions of a given topic, with little regard for the interest or ability of the students in attendance. I do not suggest that these trainers are merely egomaniacs who seek the spotlight with an intention to bore students; I believe that it is a matter of simple lack of training about the significant, highly pertinent field of adult learning research and how to use this research to make training interesting. Training others requires creativity and a degree of panache, as well as establishing rapport with the audience, some risk-taking, and, finally, earning (and keeping) the attention and interest of the audience. We must endeavor to reach a higher standard of education in law enforcement, and this journey begins with a better understanding of adult learning styles.

Several thousand years ago, the philosopher Confucius identified a simple truth with regard to the attainment of understanding. As he stated so simply, in order to understand a method, one must first do it. Thus, there are essentially three categories of learners: visual, auditory, and kinesthetic learners. No one type is inherently better, smarter, or more competent than the others. The three types are simply categories meant to describe the learning preferences of individuals, according to their skills and abilities. Let's examine each type of learner before discussing how to conform to each learner's expectations and needs in the law enforcement classroom.

Visual Learners

Contemporary, traditional models of education heavily favor visual learners. The use of overhead projectors, slide presentations, chalkboards, books, and written materials reinforces the success of the visually oriented student. In the United States, the proliferation of television, computers, movies, and the like contribute to the development of highly refined visual-processing skills throughout our lives; conversely, in cultures where these medium are not as mainstream, human beings are often more naturally disposed to more interactive learning methods. Visual learners are highly adept at studying pictures, diagrams, and written materials to gain data, draw conclusions, and make recommendations. Like their civilian counterparts, the majority of law enforcement officers are visual learners.

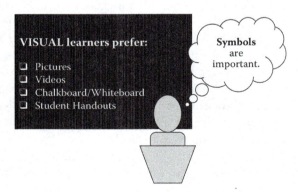

Developing instruction for visual learners is instinctual for most police trainers. The use of visually appealing slide presentations, analysis of photographs and videos, and written assignments and instructions are effective techniques for visual learners. In contrast, students who are weak in visual skills may be poor readers, miss crucial details in photographs or video presentations, or have difficulty understanding written materials that are not actually discussed.

Auditory Learners

A study of human culture over the past thousand years reveals that, before the masses were literate, the oral tradition was the primary method of transmitting knowledge. The existing framework of storytelling, folk tales, and traditional rhymes are the legacy of those traditions. A modern-day dichotomy, the auditory learner gains understanding best through listening (aural) activities. Thus, engaging in discussions, hearing about topics in detail, and associated oral methods are critical to auditory learners. Auditory learners may need to actually interact with the instructor to get the most meaning out of a topic because an auditory learner must connect with a topic through use of *language*, whereas the visual learner connects with the topic through use of *symbols* (pictures or writing).

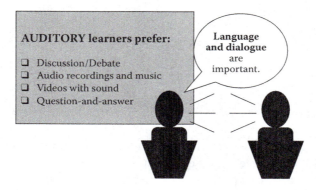

Auditory learners respond to a curriculum that incorporates music, debate, and interaction with the instructor through question-and-answer sessions. Videos with sound will be especially vibrant for aural learners, but a discussion about the video before or after viewing will be crucial to reveal the teaching points. Highly effective police training approaches for auditory learners involve the use of radio transmissions or audiotaped surveillance to illustrate a point. In comparison, students who are weak in auditory processing may be overwhelmed by extraneous or noisy classroom activities and need reinforcement to "hear" the salient points if not immediately apparent.

Kinesthetic Learners

Some students simply must physically interact with a topic to grasp it well. The law enforcement profession is highly kinesthetic (hands-on) in nature. Whether police officers are kinesthetic learners before they enter the profession or become so as a result of the job remains to be answered. It is known that recruit police officers must master a range of kinesthetic skills in the police academy — physical fitness, defensive tactics, and firearms are among several critical areas. Beyond basic training, law enforcement officers must learn to operate a motor vehicle in the line of duty under normal and emergency conditions. Driving, shooting, writing citations, and arresting activities are all hands-on. Most police officers enjoy the active quality of the profession and seek the involvement these activities provide.

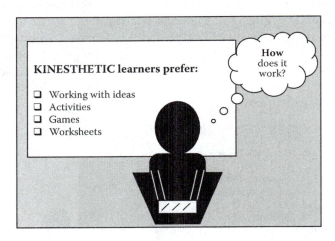

Kinesthetic learners enjoy the opportunity to work with some aspect of a topic as part of their learning experience. A dynamic instructor can provide these kinesthetic opportunities through giving students something to physically "do" or create during a class. Games and drawing activities, worksheets, use of props, and more creative means can make a critical difference for the kinesthetic learner; the difference between seeing and hearing about handcuffs and getting to physically manipulate the handcuffs is crucial. Conversely, kinesthetically challenged students will shy away from hands-on activities. Predictably, students who are unskilled in hands-on activities are few in the law enforcement profession, due to the high demands for competency in these skills during basic training.

A Study in Techniques

Thus, the question is, How does a law enforcement trainer develop training that incorporates preferred learning activities for each type of learner? The answer is through the application of a systematic process at the initial stages of development. First, plan the content of the topic with all learners in mind. Consider what visual, auditory, and kinesthetic techniques can be used for each objective. Next, develop structured lessons that will appeal to each learner style. Put in simple terms, present each teaching point in three separate-but-equal ways whenever possible.

Let's examine this process in action. Imagine that a new training need is identified at your police department. With the assistance of subject-matter experts, three objectives are developed:

Topic: Domestic Violence
At the conclusion of this course, the student will ...
1. Explain the definition of domestic violence.
2. Describe three common symptoms of abusive relationships.
3. Cite the existing departmental policy for mandatory arrest in a domestic violence incident.

Beginning with Objective 1, we must identify different techniques to train the audience to develop a thorough understanding of this definition. Unlike the traditional approach, which emphasizes lecture, rote memorization, and passive training, we will involve the audience actively in the learning experience. Thus, the initial question is, What visual, auditory, and kinesthetic techniques can we employ for each objective?

Beyond the Slide Show: Visual Techniques

Recall that visual techniques include the use of videos, pictures, and written materials. A basic familiarity with popular movies can provide a wealth of training materials for police instructors addressing the needs of visual learners. Brief but powerful movie clips can set the stage for a lesson in a dramatic, entertaining way. Many trainers use video clips to communicate deeper concepts. In general, United States copyright law is not generally breeched when video and photographic materials are used by public safety trainers in a non-revenue-generating environment. In other words, if your department is not seeking a profit from training endeavors, you can utilize movie clips and the like by simply giving proper citation (or "credit where credit is due") to the copyright owner. Just to ensure compliance with the law, acquaint your training staff with the laws governing "fair use" of public domain items, such as those acquired on the Internet.*

Beginning with the desire for insightful visual materials, I would consider my existing knowledge of domestic violence in the media. Without conducting any research, one powerful Hollywood version of the reality of domestic

---

* For more complete guidance on fair use, consult your personal attorney or department's legal counsel.

violence that comes to mind involves the violent relationship between music legends Ike and Tina Turner. Another case that I recall involves a female dentist who repeatedly ran over her husband when she caught him with another woman in the parking lot of a hotel. This Texas homicide was especially memorable because it was highly publicized and caught on videotape. Yet a third incident of recent memory involves a prominent pop singer and her boyfriend involved in a violent confrontation and subsequent arrest; these cases are a constant occurrence and provide endless fodder for training use. Most police trainers have some recollection of similar cases or their Hollywood equivalents. Use this personal knowledge to begin your development of a striking visual presentation.

Another visual approach might be the use of domestic violence photographs. Most police departments maintain photographs of victims for prosecution purposes. Inquire as to whether these items might be used for training purposes. It is important to note, however, that true victims should be protected from unwanted identification, even to a law enforcement audience. If necessary, secure permission to use the photographs from the victim or show photos that do not include the victim's face or potential identifying marks (i.e., distinctive tattoos). Alternately, cut and paste a photograph into a slide presentation and then use the draw toolbar to insert a black stripe over the eyes of the victim to conceal his or her identity.

Advanced development of slide presentations for law enforcement is a field unto itself. As a perpetual novice of this art, I personally seek the input of more skilled developers when using slide presentation tools. If tastefully employed, animation, color, and other features can add a dimension of interest to your presentations. However, I offer this statement with a word of caution. Some experts have rightfully observed that slide presentations in the wrong hands have been one of the most ineffective methods of training delivery ever developed, setting the profession back years in skills development and substance. So many police trainers use slide presentations as both a crutch and notes guide, reading from the slides items that the audience can read for themselves. Contrary to popular use, this is not the intended purpose of slide presentation software.

As a matter of policy for all trainers, I suggest a "cold turkey" approach to the use of slide presentations in the classroom. Utilize a well-written lesson plan with full instructor notes to give your class structure instead of a slide presentation. Barring the ability to abstain entirely from slide presentation use, strictly forgo the use of slides that have any more than ten words per slide. Edit the slides you cannot do without to conform to this ten-word limit. Use of more simple techniques, like photographs and videos, will add to the learning experience of the visual learner in remarkable ways that typical slide presentations cannot.

Hearing What Is Said: Auditory Techniques

Next, we must consider the auditory learners. What materials can we use to engage this set of students? Remember that some materials are cross-preferential, in that more than one type of learner will benefit from them. For example, a video with sound will be just as effective for both visual *and* auditory learners. Initially, just as with the visual learners, I suggest consulting the trainer's own memory for notorious, unusual, or striking events — whether local, Hollywood, or personal in nature.

In keeping with our domestic violence example, one set of audio recordings that is unforgettable for many is the documented violent relationship between the athlete-turned-actor O.J. Simpson and his murdered wife, Nicole Simpson. Obviously, the use of audiotaped 9-1-1 calls and radio transmissions can be immensely successful with aural students. Many of these examples can be located using an Internet search or in existing department records. Second only to these original sources, the reading aloud of an actual call or event can also be dynamic and interesting, if practiced in a dramatic way beforehand. Consider also the use of a skit to demonstrate a domestic violence situation. For the aural learners, remember that the actual dialogue used is extremely important; focus on key words, clear delivery, and effective voice projection.

Music is another powerful technique to use with auditory learners. One of the most unforgettable presentations I have ever seen on domestic violence fused popular music with images of domestic violence victims. As the images faded in and out, The Police's "Every Breath You Take" played (no pun intended). At the conclusion of this dramatic montage of images and music, the presenter explained that the origin of the song was unknown to most people. By the songwriter's own admission, "Every Breath You Take" was borne out of his rage and frustration at his estranged wife during their separation and subsequent divorce. Although no domestic violence occurred in this relationship, the use of music to teach a relevant point is a creative and memorable experience for both the student and instructor.

Interaction through discussion is also a crucial component for auditory-oriented students to fully learn material in a meaningful way. Are there "bones of contention" that can be explored as an impromptu debate between student and instructor or among students themselves? I suggest trainers explore issues of controversy existing in domestic violence situations. For example, do the students believe that women should be arrested as often as men when they commit violence in the home? Even when small children are present? Do students agree that many women may initiate abuse by hitting their partners first or do they believe that this is a myth?

Engaging students in a moderated debate is one of the most underrepresented techniques in law enforcement training. I believe this is due to the lack of comfort with conflict in the classroom felt by most police trainers. Because it is our job as police officers to control situations in the field, we feel uncomfortable with loosening the reins and exploring other viewpoints than our own, even in safer environments like the classroom.* Under carefully constructed circumstances, a lively debate can invigorate auditory learners, some of whom will take leadership of debate opportunities, whereas visual and kinesthetic learners will generally assume a more passive role. Auditory learners who do not participate in the discussion will still acquire knowledge from listening to the arguments, even if they do not actively participate. It is in the use of language to describe the concept that auditory learners grow in their understanding.

Feeling the Gist: Kinesthetic Techniques

Last, we must develop structured activities for the kinesthetic learners. Kinesthetic audiences are often restless as they wait for the visual and auditory techniques to be presented. Though they may enjoy videos, debate, and pictures for their own sake, especially if they can participate, inherently they want something to do while they learn. Games and worksheets are enjoyable for kinesthetic learners because there is an active component of participation.

In general, activities that lead to movement and motion are going to be most palatable to the kinesthetic student. Constructing situations that require a volunteer from the audience, like a role-play or scribe function, will assist the instructor in getting kinesthetic learners engaged with the topic. Alternately, small group work can be stimulating for both the auditory and kinesthetic learners, especially if problem solving or a written decision of some kind is needed. Send the students to a group activity and observe who writes things down and you will have likely identified the kinesthetic and visual learners. Conversely, the auditory learner will often not even bring a pen to the group.

To truly reach the kinesthetic learners, aim to increase the active portion of class through combination activities that piggyback multiple tasks. Recall that we have been referring to the domestic violence example. One option could direct students to a small group activity that requires the students to

---

* The greatest potential pitfall in the use of debate is loss of control of the interaction, due to the constant presence of strong personalities in our profession. Experience is the best teacher of this frangible skill. I suggest a careful review of effective facilitation guidelines before utilizing this technique for the first time with police audiences.

develop a skit on the right and the wrong way to handle domestic violence calls. Not only are you keeping the students active by encouraging group synthesis, you are asking for a creative product to be *demonstrated* in the end, not just discussed or debated. Keeping kinesthetic learners busy "doing" is the key to success. These hands-on students will also benefit from anything they can touch. Handing around photographs, weapons that have been made safe, or other props can be highly effective.

Bringing It All Together

After taking the time to include all types of learners — visual, auditory, and kinesthetic — you will have the beginnings of a great course, characterized by student activity. Your initial development may now look something like this:

Topic: Domestic Violence
Objectives: At the conclusion of this course, the student will ...
1. Explain the definition of domestic violence.
   Visual: Show video clip A [Tina and Ike Turner movie].
   Auditory: Play six-minute 9-1-1 tape [Case #123]. Discuss.
   Kinesthetic: Hand out photos [Smith case].
2. Describe three common symptoms of abusive relationships.
   Visual: Show photos 1-10 [victims] and 11-13 [suspects].
   Auditory: Play "Every Breath You Take" montage. Discuss.
   Kinesthetic: Students role-play arrest situation (right vs. wrong way).
3. Cite the existing departmental policy for mandatory arrest in a domestic violence incident.
   Visual: Slide presentation and handout policy 1-A.
   Auditory: Debate whether the departmental policy is fair ("bone of contention").
   Kinesthetic: Perform skit of mock domestic violence and have student complete worksheet and arrest report.

Now, we have a real starting point to begin development of a plan for a dynamic police training course. All learner types have been considered in the initial conceptualization of this course. We have rejected a lecture-based instructional method and incorporated a variety of materials. Using this approach, we will keep the boring discourse to a minimum and maximize interaction with and between the students. Though we still must state, write, and train to the definitions, policies, and other details, if we utilize a vibrant approach to the delivery, the returns are multiplied by a large degree because the students drive the learning process. Instead of a strict focus on the instructor and what he or she has to say, this class is designed to facilitate interaction with and by the students. This is a course that, by its very design, will be interesting and stimulating to attend, even for veteran police officers.

Unfortunately, there are always exceptions to the rule. Under certain circumstances, it may not be possible to address all three preferences for every objective. Strive for consistency in your development efforts, if not in your actual results.

A Revision Challenge

At this point, make a thorough examination of any existing course in your repertoire beginning with objectives only. Discard the existing slide presentation and materials and build learning strategies to meet the objectives using a variety of visual, auditory, and kinesthetic techniques to invigorate the students. Once armed with this new arsenal, distill the crucial elements of the training down to their very origins and keep only what is necessary to educate the audience. Focus less on the process of using typical materials and more on the selection of thought-provoking kernels of wisdom; lessen the time spent "going through the motions" and increase the time spent on more ground-breaking techniques of delivery. Thus liberated, emphasize creativity in the classroom and observe the results for yourself.

Understanding the three preferences of adult learners is a key to success in classroom. Each type of learner has advantages and disadvantages and, oftentimes, people have the ability to learn in multiple ways. Using a variety of approaches to teach the same concept to different people within the profession will energize students and develop the trainer's ability to communicate concepts of increasing complexity and relevance to law enforcement audiences.

Law Enforcement Curriculum Development Overview

5

Discipline is the bridge between goals and accomplishment.
—**Jim Rohn**

While providing training to police instructors over the years, I have discovered two primary areas of difficulty in achieving success in developing classroom training programs. The first area involves understanding the proper format for writing clear and measurable performance objectives. The second area is cultivation of the ability to write lesson plans that are complete, finished works. This chapter will provide an introduction to the basic structure for both of these crucial areas and make them achievable, manageable goals for law enforcement trainers. We will accomplish these goals through discipline and the use of simple terms to demystify these key curriculum development concepts.

Let's begin by exploring the basic construction of performance objectives. Consider that a lesson plan itself provides the framework for an intellectual adventure for students, led by you, the instructor. If a lesson plan is a journey, the objectives are the road map. After all, before you can plan a journey, you must have a road map of where you would like to go. For example, you cannot reach the destination of the great pyramids at Giza without first traveling to Egypt. You may know that it is east of you and in the Sahara Desert, but you are not equipped to arrive there without a definitive plan — including airline tickets, a passport, and the like. Can you take a journey without a map? Absolutely, you can, but the difference between a planned and unplanned journey is the expectation of a specific outcome or final goal.

Objectives provide the map of the territory into which you will venture as an instructor. When developed correctly, they will not only provide directions to the destination, they will allow the use of the most efficient route to get there. With a well-designed lesson plan, not only will you be able to get to your intended destination, you will be able to intellectually transport the students there as well.

Qualities of Police Performance Objectives

Performance objectives are the absolute, nonnegotiable beginning point of all lesson plans in development. This point cannot be emphasized too strongly.

Instructors who conversely begin with the slide presentation need remedial training in adult education principles. Creating a slide presentation (visual aid) without a lesson plan (road map) is like filling up a photograph album with pictures *before* you have taken a trip. You cannot know what visual aids you will need in your course until you determine what you will teach to the students. Therefore, always begin with performance objectives as the skeleton framework for your ideas.

What are objectives and how are they used? Objectives have three basic qualities — they are student focused, unbiased, and measurable. Let's explore each quality, independently.

Objectives Are Student Focused

The primary question to ask when constructing performance objectives is both simple and straightforward. What do I want the student to be able to do when he completes my course? Commonly, instructors erroneously write objectives that articulate what the *instructor* will do, instead of what the *student* will be able to do.

Incorrect:
Objective 1 — Introduce students to three major street gangs.
Objective 2 — Demonstrate how gang initiations are conducted.

Using the above objectives, the expectation of student performance and participation is not clear. No learning road map is actually present, only a rudimentary outline of the process that will be used to structure the class. The instructor knows what *he* wants to do in this block of instruction. He wants to inform the students about three types of gangs and wants to show videos of gang initiations, but he is not certain what role, if any, the *students* will play in the educational process. This is a colossal mistake. Taken quite literally from a professional educator's viewpoint, the instructor has written objectives that will measure learning by having students demonstrate gang initiations at the conclusion of the course.

Objectives should always be geared toward student performance, not instructor actions. In many cases, it is easiest to use a simple introductory phrase to help instructors remember that the objectives must always be *student focused*, not instructor focused.

Correct:
At the conclusion of this training, the student will ...
Objective 1 — Identify three major street gangs.
Objective 2 — Explain how gang initiations are conducted.

The addition of this short modifier ("At the conclusion of this training, the student will …") changes the language of the objective to focus on the behavior of the student. This is the student-centered principle of performance objectives development.

Objectives Are Unbiased and Measurable

Next, we must construct performance objectives according to a standard free from instructor bias. Instructors are human beings and will bring certain perspectives to any curriculum they design. As such, in order to meet this standard, a careful analysis of the language used in the objective must be conducted to ensure that no trace of our subjectivity remains.

This process sounds more complicated than it really is. In fact, the language of bias is easy to identify. Certain words and phrases are indicative of bias in an objective. Let's examine several examples of this language in action:

Incorrect:
The student will … *properly* disassemble a Sig Sauer P226 handgun.

Is there a set standard of "properness" that can be measured in a rational, objective way? The answer to this question is, equivocally, no. Objectives must be free from language like *proper* because each instructor will perceive this standard a little (or a lot) differently. Likewise, how can the degree of properness actually be measured? An astute observer once characterized police work as merely "shades of gray." I agree. There is no authoritative guide for propriety in police work, either in the field or in the academy. Therefore, I suggest another approach to writing objectives that removes the bias imposed by proper standards.

To illustrate this principle in another way, imagine instead the trickier standard of determining the proper field interview, the proper handcuffing method, or the proper defensive tactic response to a resisting subject. Again, there are degrees of properness in response and many ways to accomplish these objectives successfully. We must strive to write the objective to conform to a reasonably unchanging standard or frame of reference. In the case of firearms, a written standard already exists. Hence, the objective can be rewritten:

Correct:
The student will … disassemble a Sig Sauer P226 handgun according to the manufacturer's specifications, as listed in Sig Sauer Armorer Handbook XYZ.

If an objective can be qualified with other indicators, name them within the objective itself. For example:

Incorrect:
    The student will … *properly* demonstrate a field interview stance.
Correct:
    The student will … demonstrate a field interview, using tact, physical control techniques, and a bladed (gun side away) interview stance.

This revised objective clearly identifies the areas of importance for this task — namely, tact, subject control, and a specific body position that is needed. Contrast this criterion with the term properly and notice the huge disparity in potential interpretation by the instructor.

The same principle applies to the terms *acceptable* or *appropriate*. These terms introduce the potential for vastly different standards among instructors and student performance. Avoid these terms or define them very specifically within the lesson plan.

Another example of bias language can be found in the following example:

Incorrect:
    The student will … explain the reasons for the use of deadly force, *to the satisfaction of the instructor.*

This phraseology directs the instructor to determine, on a case-by-case basis, which students will pass or fail this objective, based on subjective observation. No real guidance is given to the instructor to determine when a student has met expectations. As classroom leaders, we cannot hold students accountable for impossible or arbitrary standards. Expectations must be based upon stated criterion, and an instructor's mere opinion is not necessarily explicit or reliable. Rewritten below, this standard becomes measurable.

Correct:
    The student will… explain the reasons for the use of deadly force, *in accordance with XYZ Police Department General Order 123.*

Tying the objectives to departmental policy is a smart, strategic decision. In this way, training conforms to written policy and an instructor's personal liability can be minimized.

Police Training Lesson Plans: Basics

In the past four chapters, we have explored the relevancy and need for diversified and sound training programs in law enforcement education. Although there are a number of approaches to dynamic delivery, or the "how to" portion of training, we must first learn the secret intricacies of lesson plan preparation — how to write what we will teach. After developing clear objectives, the next step is the writing of the lesson plan.

Writing lesson plans is one of the most difficult aspects of the curriculum development process, especially for police trainers. This is not a blanket indictment of the abilities or limitations of police trainers in general but is simply a logical conjecture based on my experience. I believe it is merely a symptom of the greater ill that plagues police training programs, in general. The failure of departments to prepare trainers to actually use (rather than simply hear about) a template of the adult education process leads to their inability to create dynamic training programs. Without a staff of skilled, resident developers, many departments look elsewhere for competent professional guidance. Generally, a common solution to the training need is the employment of non-police educators to write programs to be delivered by experienced law enforcement officers. This approach, though likely to result in measurable objectives and a well-written lesson plan, will be functionally blind to the unique preferences, interests, and needs of the police audience.

The development of truly insightful, rigorous, and complex training programs for police officers must be trusted to those who have worn the badge and done the job. It is far easier to make a police officer into a teacher than to make a teacher into a police officer. Time and again I have seen a well-intentioned civilian instructor learn a very painful lesson in the police training environment. A fundamental misunderstanding of the lifestyles, worldviews, and personalities of police professionals creates a hostile venue for the uninitiated. Without this critical "police-centric" perspective, programs developed by our civilian counterparts have no true credibility for law enforcement audiences and will be received with lukewarm enthusiasm, under the best circumstances. One colleague called the police environment a "closed culture," and many prominent writers in the field agree.

In contrast, police-centric programs receive overwhelming interest and support of law enforcement trainers. The success of Street Survival® seminars delivered by Calibre Press, San Francisco, and the investigative techniques workshops given by John E. Reid & Associates, Chicago, among others, illustrate the degree of excellence that is possible in police training endeavors. The success of these organizations demonstrates the unprecedented need for programs developed *by police* and *for police*. Given an overview of essential elements of adult education, most police trainers can become skilled authors of law enforcement lesson plans. With this understanding, let's introduce the fundamental maxims of law enforcement curriculum design, using police-oriented language.

Lesson 1: The "Four Corners" Rule

Former students of United States constitutional law in the police academy will recall the so-called four corners rule for the issuance of search warrants. This rule postulates that all of the information that is needed for a search and seizure warrant will be contained in the four corners of the document. The same truth applies to lesson plans. All of the information needed to teach the course must be present within the lesson plan itself. The lesson plan is a living document that, like the Constitution, can and will grow over time, but its properties must remain the same. It must always be a *comprehensive* document that contains all of the information that any qualified instructor needs to teach the course.

One of the most neglected means of achieving the four corners standard is defining or eliminating technical and slang terms. How? Let's examine a case in point. If a trainer is developing a class on interpreting hits using computer-based data searches, the term *Soundex hit* might be used in the lesson plan to describe a hit that is a potential, though not exact, match. Although instructors may be generally familiar with this term, it is important to define it within the four corners of the lesson plan. Why? The answer is this: because a student may ask for the specific definition and the instructor should be able to articulate the correct answer by referring to the lesson plan.

Acronyms, slang, and police jargon can cloud learning objectives and confuse fellow instructors. I have seen written lesson plans that used terms that are undefined or subject to interpretation — terms like *dope fiend, 10-26, the posse, squirrel witness, throw-down gun, P-O-P ticket*, and *CYA* — to elucidate key teaching points. Lesson plan terminology must always be clear and unbiased. When developing a topic with unfamiliar language, ask yourself this question: Is this technical or slang terminology critical to the students' understanding of this topic? If the answer is yes, define the term in the lesson plan through a short instructor note. To ensure uniformity in training, include an asterisk (*) after the use of the technical or slang term and provide a short explanation for the instructor notes:

Example: The students may see Soundex* hits, in addition to actual search matches. Soundex hits require additional review by the student for relevance.

Instructor Note: Soundex hit is defined as a potential, but not exact match; also called a "sound-alike" match.

It is true that law enforcement is a profession filled with jargon. As instructors, we must be sure that the meaning of the jargon used in lesson plans is clear to all fellow trainers over time. Police trainers occasionally include language in lesson plans that may be unfamiliar to other instructors, even within the same department or unit. A simple way to ensure that a lesson plan does not contain any unfamiliar terms is to allow a civilian to review the lesson plan once it is fully developed. An administrative assistant, secretary, or other non-police coworker can generally proofread a lesson plan and provide input on what terminology is unclear.

Remember, all police officers were civilians once. Many, if not all, of your academy students will bring a civilian's mindset and knowledge of jargon to class. Using this approach, confusion is minimized and the lesson plan retains its comprehensive nature, regardless of the audience.

Additionally, have some references and sources for your instruction. It is true that experience is a great teacher, especially in police work. In fact, real street-level experience may be the only important differentiation between a veteran officer and a rookie. However, instruction is not simply an opportunity for you to talk about your own narrow experience. Research broadens your perspective and rounds out the street cop's education. Acquaint yourself with what information is out there and, if the information you have is not a part of the body of knowledge available, start thinking about how to get your work published, so that others can benefit from your experience.

Lesson 2: Portability

Lesson plans must be portable, meaning that they can be picked up and carried to the classroom in a simple, self-contained manner. This standard requires organization, in the form of a notebook to contain the lesson plan itself, instructor guide, participant handouts, and any multimedia items (i.e., CD, DVD). Absolute portability means that an instructor can literally pick up the lesson plan and walk into the classroom, without delay.

Often, police trainers who have worked hard to develop good training materials can become quite proprietary about their presentations. We must stop refusing to share our creative, best works with our fellow trainers. Sharing our successes as trainers and developers can multiply the talent in our profession through inspiration, leadership, and mentoring. In 2008, I enjoyed just such an experience. I had the privilege of attending a physical fitness trainer certification course hosted by the Prince George's County (Maryland) Police Department. During the course, I was educated in a way that I expected, through lecture and examination. It was only after the end of the hosted course that I received a real education in dynamic physical fitness training. A fellow trainer took me and my cohorts through a lengthy hands-on demonstration of the techniques he was currently using to challenge the recruits under his command. The trainer was a peer, yet he shared all of his wisdom, passion, and lessons learned as to the value of the full range of techniques, equipment, and results he had developed over the course of several years. Imagine the sheer excitement that the trainers who attended this impromptu session felt to experience such generosity and openness from a fellow instructor. The results were heartfelt and memorable.

Devise a system, if it does not already exist, for functional portability for lesson plans. If needed, involve fellow instructors in the redesign of worn-out methods of storing and retrieving lesson plans. Materials should be accessible on paper as well as electronically to ensure that a computer or other equipment failure does not prevent you from being able to teach a particular course.

Lesson 3: Anonymity

Anonymity means devoid of any personal agenda. Put simply, there is no place for you, specifically, within the lesson plan itself. Hence, if the lesson plan is rife with references to the writer's personal self or experiences (for example, "Tell students about involvement with XYZ case"), it does not meet the criterion for anonymity.

This suggestion does not aim to discourage the use of references to actual cases. Use of a specific case study is a wonderful classroom technique; however, the lesson plan must include all of the information that *any* instructor needs to present the information, not simply the internal memory of a *specific* instructor. Internet searches can provide important details of a specific or infamous case, which can then be printed and cited in the lesson plan, as in the following:

> Example: The Oklahoma City Bombing* was a landmark case of domestic terrorism.
> *Instructor Note: See Oklahoma City Bombing reference document in Appendix A of lesson plan.*

An instructor can also choose to include a copy of a specific police report in the lesson plan reference material, if needed. As a third option, some authors may want to give the presenting instructor some freedom to decide what personal example is relevant to the course. This alternative allows for personal interjection in the addition of an instructor note, like this example:

> *Instructor Note: Relate a police critical incident debriefing that is personally known to the instructor.*

The lesson plan must not be merely stage dressing for a specific trainer to impose his or her personal opinions, qualifications, "war stories," or politics. Under the worst circumstances, slide presentations have been developed as a crude mouthpiece for a specific instructor's experiences. These slide shows are anything but anonymous. To illustrate this point, imagine a scenario in which you must present Detective Smith's course on sexual harassment. This presentation is quickly derailed by the introductory slides delineating the high points of Smith's career, training, and awards. Predict your comfort level in presenting a slide show that also contains multiple photographs of Smith, random cartoons, and irreverent, inflammatory videos. Even slides meant to be humorous may be misinterpreted or inappropriate. Save the personal introductions, humorous anecdotes, and other such minutiae for each instructor to introduce and resolve individually.

Conclusion

In the final analysis, understand that there is a crucial difference between *delivery* of training and *development* of training. Without an adequate, fully rendered lesson plan, an effective trainer becomes nothing less than the ever-present and irreplaceable presenter; he is essentially tied to the podium, indefinitely. Put another way, if delivery is the perpetual focus of a trainer's existence, he cannot focus on development of new training materials.

By way of comparison, consider the dichotomy between the principles of management and of leadership. Management is concerned with efficiency, timeliness, and progress; leadership is the study of how we achieve those goals effectively, with a deep, philanthropic consideration of strength and weaknesses of the human beings we inspire to greatness. The fine distinction between focusing on delivery (classroom time) and development (preparation time) is also quite striking. If the goal of excellence in training is to produce measurable, replicable results, no instructor can be deemed absolutely essential to a program's success. Thus, well-written lesson plans enable departments to extract the talent and experience of its best educators, using each instructor's own intrinsic expertise; translate this experience to paper; and commit it to the institutional memory of the training program.

Recall the true value of excellence in training. I suggest that, if you have developed a quality course, you should share this course with the world of law enforcement in as large of an audience as possible. Professional associations, such as the International Law Enforcement Educators and Trainers Association (ILEETA), the International Association of Directors of Law Enforcement Standards and Training (IADLEST), and the International Association of Chiefs of Police (IACP), exist to promote your work through collaborative online communities, for the benefit of other trainers. Educate your peers whenever possible, so that others can grow in their understanding of your particular vein of expertise. Any topic in which you have personal expertise, whether it is in accident reconstruction, domestic violence, or physical fitness, can become a fully portable, dynamic training course. Encourage cross-training of staff in various areas of expertise.

Finally, suggest the idea of hosting a training conference at your agency. Alternatively, take your class on the road, to one of the many law enforcement training conferences that are held throughout the country, and give it the exposure it deserves. Then, distribute your course materials openly and genuinely to the participants, so they may utilize your course to educate others. When law enforcement trainers can develop professional working relationships, everyone involved in the police education process can benefit.

Six Levels of Understanding
Police Cognitive Skills Training

6

The sad truth is: great talent is not enough.

—Robert Kiyosaki

Influential, talented educators have long understood the relationship between challenging students to actively participate in the learning process and an increased retention of knowledge by the students. Especially with police officers, if instruction is not engaging, the class will be exceptionally long and painful. Many instructors incorporate interesting activities in their lessons instinctively. This natural inclination to engage students sets excellent instructors apart from their peers. However, it is not only talent that creates opportunities for excellence. As with any creative endeavor, natural ability is certainly nice to have, but it is not the only route to success. Competency, whether in writing, making money, or teaching, can be learned through the study of effective techniques, strategies, and other people's success stories. This chapter begins the study of an extremely successful technique that has been widely used in educational settings for many years.

We have already ascertained that a curriculum begins with the careful construction of performance objectives. Depending on the language and activities used, classes can be designed to be taught at many levels. At the most basic level, trainers can ask students to memorize a set of rules or guidelines and then test accordingly. Using this approach, students learn to regurgitate information that has little or no meaning for them personally. They can select the correct answer from a list with a limited understanding of the implications of their choices. As a result, they test and subsequently forget their experience in the classroom. This type of training is the *basic* level of instruction.

When developing training at an advanced level, instructors can lead students to actually internalize the underlying principles for rules, laws, and techniques. Instructing at an advanced level allows trainers to encourage the student's understanding of *how* and *why* to utilize instruction in his or her day-to-day work. This distinction between teaching at the basic level and at the advanced level is crucial. Focusing on actual skills development rather than passive listening and repeating is the difference between a dynamic classroom experience and a commonplace one. Truly, police work is a skills-based profession; the difference between understanding use of force and employing use of force can be a life-or-death distinction in our line of work. Police trainers want to develop skills in their students but are not often in possession of the curriculum they need to accomplish this mission.

Applying Bloom's Taxonomy

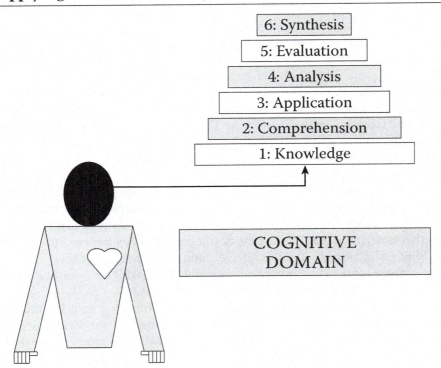

The purpose of this book is to encourage police trainers to develop their own abilities to commit to a higher standard in training design. Pursuant to that goal, we need to engender a broad understanding of a widely used adult education tool called *Bloom's taxonomy*. What is Bloom's taxonomy? For over fifty years, Bloom's taxonomy has been a system used by the educational community to guide teachers in the development of student performance objectives. The taxonomy is a continuum, categorizing student actions from lower level competency to higher capability. This tool encapsulates the learning experience into a manageable hierarchy that is a clear reference for educators. Police instructors can use this tool themselves, beginning immediately, once they understand how to apply it to the needs of our profession.

Some instructors may be skeptical of using Bloom's taxonomy. They may ask themselves: How is this "academic" method really going to be useful in my classroom? The answer is simpler than it might appear. Let's examine an illustration of the Bloom principles in action.

Police officers must *know* the laws and *comprehend* why they exist. They must *apply* their skills on the street. They must be able to *analyze* situations and decide on a course of action to protect themselves and the public. They must be able to *evaluate* a threat posed by a subject or situation; in most cases, the situations encountered will be entirely new and unpredictable. Over time, officers *create* an approach to policing that conforms to their own understanding of the role of police officers in society. These italicized terms above denote the most succinct descriptions of the six cognitive learning levels — knowledge, comprehension, application, analysis, evaluation, and synthesis — as defined by the most modern version of Bloom's taxonomy.*

Bloom's research and resulting publications on the process of education as a definable system led to widespread acceptance of his methodology in the field of education. What is useful about Bloom's taxonomy for the police educator is that it can be used to encourage greater skills development for students. Using this system, trainers can begin to create training that underscores the knowledge that there is a huge difference between a student who can choose correct answers on a written test versus one who can demonstrate a technique, explain a concept in detail, or defend his or her actions as a police officer.

Police trainers are a savvy bunch of observers, instinctively applying Bloom's hierarchy without even being aware of it. Often, the police educators I have worked with over the years were inherently aware of whether a particular student was fit or unfit for the profession, independently of their test scores. An experienced defensive tactics instructor confided in me that he worried more about the students who were good test takers:

> ... Law enforcement is a business that you can't intellectualize your way out of. When you have a resisting suspect, discussion goes out the window ... the kids who can ace tests don't like to put their hands on someone when they should, because they want to talk or think it over first. For a cop, that attitude can get them killed. ...

Using Bloom's principles modified for law enforcement, police educators can emphasize the development of objectives that define the level of skill that is needed — whether it is basic comprehension or more complex analysis by the students. Understanding this concept, in turn, allows police academies to train to reasonable levels of mastery in students and reflect the reality of

---

* Rather than entering into a comprehensive discussion of the history of Bloom and his research conclusions, I recommend readers examine this body of work online or through the local library.

law enforcement work outside the classroom. Thus, we do not produce great test-takers. Instead, we produce competent police officers.

After all, there is no multiple-choice examination to pass on the streets. Students must be able to understand and apply concepts that are taught in the classroom. Bloom's taxonomy is the key to understanding the development of the learning process and tailoring your instruction to the proper level for the audience.

There are three subcategories, or domains, in Bloom's taxonomy: cognitive, affective, and psychomotor. Cognitive skills relate to the student's knowledge and thinking process. Affective skills are measured in terms of student's beliefs and attitudes. Psychomotor skills are concerned with hard motor skills and performance. In the words of my brilliant colleague, Mr. Eric Waldt, these domains are more easily remembered as the "head," "heart," and "hands."

Let's begin with the cognitive domain, or the head skills. This division is concerned with affecting the student's thought process, problem-solving ability, and intellectual activities. Cognitive objectives make students think, or use their cognition, to solve problems. In police-centric terms, a recruit who does not possess knowledge of laws, firearms, or defensive tactics cannot do the job of police work. Whether writing a traffic citation, firing a handgun, or performing a takedown, police officers need to know what to do, within legal, physical, and departmental limits, before they can act.

Knowledge is the cornerstone of a well-rounded education and the very lowest level of cognitive skill. When beginning the training process, some topics do require the mere cultivation of knowledge and nothing more. For example, in teaching recruits to stand at attention, what is crucial is that the student first *knows* the position that is needed to meet a drill instructor's expectations — arms at this position and feet at this position. Knowledge is also the foundation for the higher levels of learning. It is not always necessary to begin with an objective that is written at the basic level, but it is probably easiest to measure.

Cognitive Level One: Knowledge

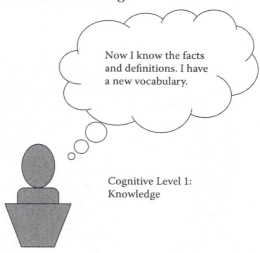

Cognitive Level 1:
Knowledge

Consider this performance objective:

At the end of this block of instruction the student will ...
    Define deadly force. [Cognitive — 1]

What is the goal of this objective? The answer: to measure basic student knowledge. Operating at this level, the student will pass if he is able to recall the definition of deadly force presented in class. The functional test of knowledge at this basic level is the ability to remember the terms that were presented, the vocabulary of the lessons. Unfortunately, in this example, mere knowledge of the terminology does not reflect the reality of the depth of what police officers need to know about deadly force. Yet, many academies are content with such lean objectives, and the students suffer the consequences when they graduate onto the streets.

Thus, understand that knowledge-based objectives are basic concepts. Cognitive objectives ask students to define, identify, list, and state information for an examination. An appropriate use of this level of training would be in support of the development of law enforcement-appropriate vocabulary terms, like *warrant, adjudication, misdemeanor,* and other terms. Also, knowledge-based objectives are used for testing the nomenclature of equipment, including the parts of firearms, handcuffs, less-lethal weapons, and uniform-issue regalia.

Cognitive Level Two: Comprehension

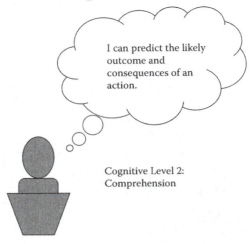

I can predict the likely outcome and consequences of an action.

Cognitive Level 2: Comprehension

At the end of this block of instruction the student will ...
Discuss the implications of using deadly force in an unauthorized manner. [Cognitive — 2]

This objective is concerned with the identification of the consequences associated with a particular behavior, namely unauthorized deadly force. At this second level, comprehension requires the student to possess basic knowledge about the concept and then outline the rational outcome of violating a policy or law. Generally, this is in the form of a verbal exercise or written examination.

Comprehending material requires more than simple rote memorization — it demands a thought process from the student to predict consequences, describe methods, and explain information that was introduced. An appropriate use of level two would be in support of key police practices and procedures. Additionally, discussions of search-and-seizure case law require comprehension of legal argument by the student, not simply knowledge.

Cognitive Level Three: Application

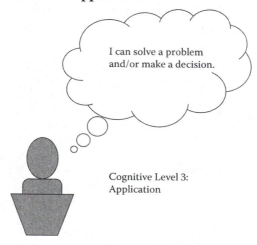

Cognitive Level 3:
Application

Application takes thinking skills to the next level, wherein students must be able to use learned materials in novel and unexpected circumstances. The difference between level two and level three is that, in level three, students will now have to use their understanding to solve a problem, develop an answer, or demonstrate their actual mastery through the creative process. At level three, students are able to enter into scenario-based learning (SBL) environments to demonstrate their knowledge and skills.*

It is crucial to understand that bringing application into the educational experience is the pivotal threshold for student retention. Allowing police students to participate in carefully constructed law enforcement scenarios is a significant, fundamental need in police training. Application-based objectives allow SBL developers and instructors to have a framework for student competence.

Now, consider the following objective:

> At the end of this block of instruction the student will ...
>> Apply deadly force in a scenario-based learning environment, using a police-issued firearm, in a manner consistent with departmental policy. [Cognitive — 3]

This objective demands student knowledge in addition to the ability to apply that knowledge to make a split-second decision regarding deadly force. Is this a relevant skill for police officers? The answer is absolutely. A student must not only understand the concept and comprehend the departmental

---

* A discussion of SBL design and development is undertaken more in-depth in a later chapter of this book.

policy — he or she must apply the knowledge appropriately, under controlled circumstances. Constructing application-based objectives ensures that a student is able to utilize his or her knowledge, separating the "book-smart" recruit from the "street-smart" officer.

Understand that this objective is not designed to assess firearms qualification ability. It is designed to measure the student's internal thought process of determining when to apply deadly force, assuming that he has a working knowledge of the policy governing his actions. If either piece is missing, he cannot complete this exercise with accuracy.

Cognitive Level Four: Analysis

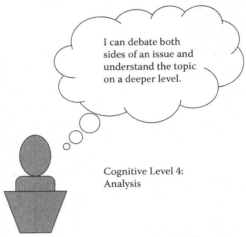

I can debate both sides of an issue and understand the topic on a deeper level.

Cognitive Level 4:
Analysis

At the end of this block of instruction the student will …
Differentiate the circumstances under which deadly force and less-than-lethal force are authorized, according to departmental policy. [Cognitive — 4]

Ask yourself: Can this objective be tested using a multiple-choice format? The answer is yes, but it will not be a simple endeavor. A case study would need to be developed, followed by a series of in-depth answers for selection by the student. In my experience, contemporary law enforcement training programs are often too closely tied to multiple-choice, computer-graded systems designed to streamline the educational process, minimizing the human factor. However, in order to test the ability of a student to analyze a problem and formulate a solution, we must be willing to undertake another method of examination.

An oft-neglected format for assessing analysis skills is ideal in this situation: the student essay. Analysis-based objectives invite the student to think deeply about an issue, using his or her own understanding, and present an argument or rationale based on that intrinsic understanding. Given that level of participation, a student will need to be truly immersed in a concept to present an analysis. This immersion can be accomplished through constructed SBL or detailed case studies of real or fictional police incidents. Analysis-based objectives are ideal for topics with multiple layers and perspectives, including use of force, criminal law, and officer survival.

Cognitive Level Five: Evaluation

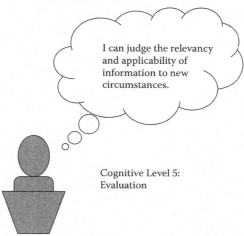

I can judge the relevancy and applicability of information to new circumstances.

Cognitive Level 5:
Evaluation

Higher levels of cognitive performance require a more active engagement of the student. At level five, the student is reaching a level of expertise with a topic that allows him to reflect on the qualitative level of performance of himself or others in a given situation. At this level, the student is entering into a new realm; he is leaving the role of a passive, desk-bound pupil and becoming an active surveyor of himself and others. Recalling the lower levels of cognitive performance, remember that level one requires mere knowledge of definitions, whereas level five now requires student commentary on the level of compliance or value of information, actions, or policies.

Consider the following:

At the end of this block of instruction the student will …
   Assess the level of compliance with departmental deadly force policy, given a detailed summary of an officer-involved use of force incident. [Cognitive — 5]

Evaluation-based objectives are highly regarded by students because they allow the students to take ownership of the learning process as active, opinioned participants. Do law enforcement officers have strong opinions about media-produced summaries of police work, whether in the newspaper, on the radio, television, or Internet? The answer is, indubitably, yes. Constructing evaluation-based objectives allows students to demonstrate mastery of a topic through intellectual discourse. These types of activities are highly enjoyable for law enforcement audiences, though occasionally quite heated and expansive in scope. Level five objectives are ideal for topics requiring a value judgment, like disciplinary structures and ethics.

Cognitive Level Six: Synthesis

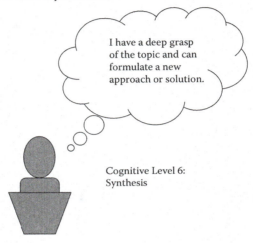

I have a deep grasp of the topic and can formulate a new approach or solution.

Cognitive Level 6: Synthesis

At the end of this block of instruction the student will …
Develop a model police department deadly force policy for nationwide use. [Cognitive — 6]

Level six objectives represent the conclusion of the student's journey in a particular topic. Once the student has mastered the lower levels, he or she is now equipped to contribute new material to the field. The student may propose a new approach to an existing problem or formulate a novel way to integrate new material with existing data. At this level, the student has mastered the knowledge, application, and analysis of information that has been presented. The student has developed his or her own opinions and value systems about the topic. Now, the student will present a new, personally creative approach or enlightened view.

In my experience, using level six objectives for law enforcement training is a rare occurrence. This is due to the fact that, inherent to the profession, creativity is not a virtue. Law enforcement work requires diligence and respect for existing schemas of policy, law, and procedure. Because we are governed by law, statute, and court cases, police officers do not regularly use personal innovation in their approach to street work. Enforcement work does not often elicit the need for creative solutions — in fact, imaginative street-level "experiments" can trigger liability claims, excessive use of force, and outcries of discrimination. However, with regard to policy-making and other executive-level functions, synthesis-based objectives *are* useful in police training. Our command staff members must be able to create and develop new and ground-breaking ideas. An excellent example of this maxim in action would be the use of level six objectives in support of training first-line supervisors or higher administrators.

Final Commentary on Cognitive Skills Training

Too often, police instructors do not recognize that students move through the six cognitive levels fluidly over time, through careful leadership. It is an exercise in frustration to attempt to have entry-level recruits master the synthesis level in any topic during the first week of police academy. Alternately, to force experienced officers through a course designed with knowledge-level rote memorization of definitions that are well known is deeply offensive. One of the most important principles of instructional systems design is to know the audience for whom the material is being developed. Thus, an audience of tenured robbery investigators brings a different niche of expertise to a class than, say, an audience of tactical paramedics or police dispatchers. The objectives must always be at the appropriate level for the audience.

One of the reasons for a universally poor experience in the police training classroom is the lack of emphasis on motivating the students to participate. Cognition-based objectives should be utilized at the higher levels whenever possible to create excitement in the learning environment. If we can move police education programs away from the focus on low levels of thinking, we can begin to challenge students to use their own skills of thought, analysis, and synthesis to contribute to the learning experience for all participants. Though a certain degree of skill is required on behalf of the instructors involved, some of this change must be made at the curriculum level. Rewriting knowledge-based (level one) objectives into analysis-based (level four) or evaluation-based (level five) objectives creates a completely new classroom experience.

For example:

- Existing Objective: Define use of force.
- Revised Objective: Explain the relationship between offender's level of resistance and authorized use of force.

This objective requires thought on the student's part. He or she must understand the information in a deeper way to explain a concept versus a simple definition.

- Existing Objective: List three principles of community-oriented policing.
- Revised Objective: Differentiate between traditional patrol and community-oriented policing approaches.

Here, we ask the student to tell us the difference, rather than regurgitating a memorized list of variables. Once again, the student must understand the concepts before he can differentiate between them.

- Existing Objective: State the departmental policy for take-home patrol vehicles.
- Revised Objective: Analyze the strengths and weaknesses of the take-home patrol vehicles policy and recommend improvements.

In this objective, we require the highest level of processing. Analyze what is, and then propose improvements.

Developing quality cognition-based objectives requires due diligence to ascertain the desired level of student understanding. Too many programs focus on the lowest levels of intellectual exercise. Police officers, whether recruits or in-service, are capable of more and should be encouraged to demonstrate their intellectual skills.

Five Levels of Internal Change
Police Affective Skills Training

7

I have always believed that 98% of a student's progress is due to his own efforts and 2% to his teacher.

—**John Philip Sousa**

John Philip Sousa was one of the greatest composers of the twentieth century. His specialty, authoring and conducting patriotic marches, made up the bulk of his career in music. Sousa was an exceptionally talented musician, in addition to his gifts as a composer. At the age of six, he began playing the violin with absolute pitch — a rare ability in a musician of any age. In the next ten years, he learned to play all of the orchestral wind instruments under the close supervision of his father, a Marine Corps Band trombonist. Sousa went on to conduct the President's own band during his illustrious career. Even today, Sousa's energetic march, "Stars and Stripes Forever," engenders a deep sense of national pride as it evokes the images of the greatest generation of American soldiers marching in military regalia.

Sousa believed that it was only necessary to achieve the right *motivation* in students to see phenomenal results. It was the ability to inspire students to seek out greatness from within, he believed, that made extraordinary progress possible. In Sousa's case, he had a tremendous talent and needed only an opportunity to express it; as a result, his music, in its very design, affected the hearts and emotions of the listener. Classroom instructors who can master this kind of leadership can teach any topic with aplomb. Thus, we begin our examination of effecting emotional change within students, using affective skills training.

Recall that affective skills are related to the development of attitudes or beliefs within the student. One example of this kind of police training is the eye-opening experience of taking an officer survival course. Whether you are a rookie officer or an experienced veteran, these courses are so high-impact and meaningful because they create a fundamental shift in one's awareness as a police officer operating on the streets.

Case in point: one of the most insightful programs I have recently seen that creates affective change is the FBI's Law Enforcement Officers Killed and Assaulted (LEOKA) course. The LEOKA presenter I had was a seasoned former police detective, Chuck Miller. Over the course of several years, Chuck traveled to the prisons where cop killers were incarcerated, usually for life. He sought the opportunity to interview these individuals about their crimes and videotaped these interviews for the LEOKA program.

What was fascinating about these interviews was the opportunity to see and hear, directly from the offender, the personal motivation these offenders had for the line-of-duty murders that they committed. Some offenders obviously had no regard for human life, least of all that of a police officer; others were momentarily ruled by the split-second determination not to go back into custody. Whatever the cause, it is absolutely an emotional moment when you hear a convicted cop killer say he took the life of a colleague in blue because the officer was distracted, overweight, or overwhelmed by circumstances. An experienced officer would detect the bravado of a "lifer" discussing how he bested our fellow officer, but the experience will move you to awareness, tinged with a great deal of anger. It is an excellent program, and I strongly urge you to attend it, if you can.

Like Chuck's work in the LEOKA program, proper instruction in affective skills saves police officers' lives. Without the commitment to survival, readiness for action, and the ability to characterize a given subject's behavior as menacing or harmless, police officers are at high risk of injury or death on the streets. Affective skills training focuses on developing the ability to notice "signs" of danger, understanding potential risks, and ingrains a value system that affirms the police culture. Thus, it is highly pertinent to police training programs.

Affective objectives create the opportunity to generate an internal change in the recruit or officer, in terms of their emotions, feelings, or beliefs. Aptly named the "heart" objectives, affective objectives "affect" students in some deep way to generate an understanding that was absent before training. For example, consider these three approaches to range safety in a firearms training course:

The instructor says, "Keep your finger off the trigger until you intend to fire."

Or

The instructor relates a story of an accidental discharge that had grave consequences then asks the students about why this event might have happened.

Or

The instructor shows videos of police officers having accidental discharges and tells students of the resulting consequences. The instructor then asks the students how these incidents could have been prevented.

The purpose of safety training for firearms is to create an attitude of respect and care and an understanding of the firearm's potential for great harm, if not handled carefully. This purpose requires an affective objective — one that will create an internal change within the student, not simply a cognitive understanding.

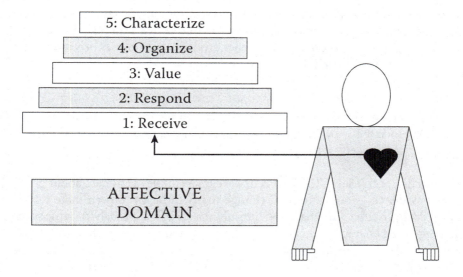

Affective Level One: Receiving Data

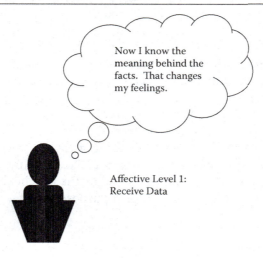

Now I know the meaning behind the facts. That changes my feelings.

Affective Level 1:
Receive Data

At the lowest level, students are asked to passively receive information or listen to opposing viewpoints. Recruits might be asked to develop an internal appreciation for a topic only, without any level of participation beyond attending to what is presented. It is a little like the topic of art appreciation — looking at lots of paintings and discussing their style but not participating in the creation of any art.

Consider, for example, a block of instruction on crime scene response. Students arrive and peer into the room where a mock crime scene has been staged, but they cannot enter. They are asked to note what they see in a small notebook. Some students may record the observation of shell casings on the floor, blood spatter on the wall, and the beer bottles with the suspect's fingerprints resting on the coffee table. Other students may not appreciate that a crime has occurred at all, if they do not recognize the signs.

Thus, the learning objective might read:

At the end of this block of instruction the student will ...
    Appreciate the existence of potential crime scene evidence in a mock crime scene setting. [Affective — 1]

Essentially, at this level, the goal is to develop a simple awareness about crime scene evidence — an attitudinal change that will begin to germinate within the recruit. In time, this change will result in a careful approach to crime scene management characterized by a concern for destruction of evidence. But, initially, police educators must focus on engendering a basic understanding of the reality that evidence does exist and that it can be seen by the trained eye.

Training courses with goals of developing sensitivity to issues of culture, race, ethnicity, and sexual orientation are other good examples of this kind of objective. However, can an instructor ever be certain that a student truly *appreciates* a racial or cultural difference? Measuring internal opinions are difficult when no active component for student participation is present. Developing a test for such a passive understanding is a challenge perhaps best met through an oral exercise, class discussion, or essay question. In our mock crime scene example, utilizing an open forum upon return to the classroom wherein students are asked to share what they saw is one approach to measuring student experience. Alternately, students could be asked to hand in their notes from the crime scene to determine individual progress.

Whenever possible, I recommend using a higher level objective that requires some aspect of student performance. Occasionally, though, simple attendance and listening are what is needed by the instructor, and level one objectives in the affective domain suit that purpose.

Affective Level Two: Responding to Data

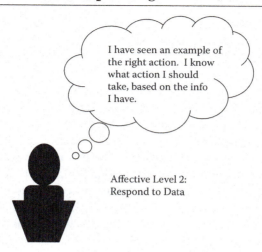

I have seen an example of the right action. I know what action I should take, based on the info I have.

Affective Level 2:
Respond to Data

At this level, we begin to require the students to participate in some way within the learning situation. This participation is governed by student understanding of or interest in the topic at hand. Thus, in addition to passively receiving information, students will now begin to act in response to the information.

The best illustrations of this type of activity are response drills conducted during entry-level defensive tactics (DT) training. Historically, understand that police recruits were not kinder and gentler people. Many had been in their share of fistfights in their teens and young adult years and may have even had minor scrapes with the law before joining the ranks. Today, our culture discourages face-to-face confrontations, preferring the safety of e-mail or phone texting, especially in the middle-class segment of society. In many cases, recruits now enter the police academy with no experience in physical confrontation *whatsoever*.*

As a result, DT instructors must begin with basic awareness drills and programming for the true self-defense novice. Different from the psychomotor skills that are discussed later, affective skills are more complicated to define in that they are characterized by attitudes, beliefs, and motivations, not hard skills delivery on the mats.

---

* A study conducted via anonymous intake surveys revealed over 80 percent of recruits had never been in a physical altercation or fistfight prior to beginning a defensive tactics program in the police academy. Although there may be some validity issues due to student apprehension over self-reporting, it is possible that this reflects an accurate view of contemporary police recruits.

Consider, for example, the following affective objective:

At the end of this block of instruction the student will …
  Respond to a noncompliant suspect with strong, verbal commands.
    [Affective — 2]

I think that all instructors would agree that the ability to respond to stimuli, especially dangerous stimuli, is a key competency for police officers. It is an unfortunate truth that some police academies never teach their students to give loud, clear verbal commands to suspects. Although this may be because of concerns over political correctness, I believe this is because administrators have forgotten that an effective command presence is something that is developed through training and diligence. Recruits are not ready to command others when they enter the academy, unless they have a military background. We must teach them to respond appropriately to diverse and unpredictable circumstances through well-designed training. Specifically, we must develop affective objectives that reinforce attitude development and change in awareness within the students.

This objective pairs a student's awareness of noncompliance with a specific *response* expected from the student — strong, verbal commands. Therefore, the student must see the behavior (level one) and do something about it, making this a level two objective.

Affective Level Three: Valuing Data

I can set priorities based on the data I have.

Affective Level 3:
Value Data

Success at this middle level of instruction requires the development of an understanding of data and how important the data is in relation to other factors. An ideal police-centric illustration requiring this type of reasoning would be the following exercise:

> You and your partner conduct a traffic stop. You are approaching the vehicle when your partner is suddenly shot by the driver of the vehicle. He falls to the ground while the suspect drives away. Do you stay with your partner to administer first aid or leave him behind to pursue the suspect?

Many renditions of this exercise are used during oral board interviews for police recruiting or in the academy to assess judgment. In this type of exercise, the emphasis is on determining the applicant's value system. Do they value saving the life of their partner or the need for apprehension of the suspects above all else? And how will they defend their choice?

Valuing objectives seek to confirm the establishment of the appropriate belief system with the student. Of course, appropriateness is relative to the situation and departmentally defined values. Let's examine this principle in action with regard to use of force. A police officer must become thoroughly familiar with his department's use of force policy before graduation. Painfully, this process usually consists of rote memorization of the various levels — for example, "soft empty hand," "impact weapon," and "deadly force" are different levels of force. However, students must also be able to determine when each of the levels is authorized. Value-based objectives allow us to test the student's internal beliefs, relative to what we, the instructors, have determined is important.

For example:

> At the end of this block of instruction the student will …
> > Demonstrate an awareness of the levels of the use of force continuum and when they are authorized, according to departmental standards. [Affective — 3]

Internally, the dialogue within the student should address these types of questions:

> "Is _____ an appropriate level of force in this particular situation?"
> "What use of force action should I take based on _____?"

Students who can successfully answer these questions have developed a baseline set of values at this objective level.

Affective Level Four: Organizing Data

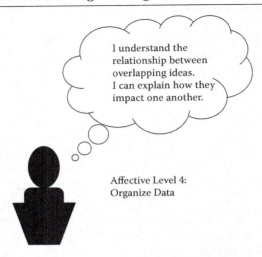

I understand the relationship between overlapping ideas. I can explain how they impact one another.

Affective Level 4:
Organize Data

Organizing objectives take values-based attitudes to the next level. Not only must a student now hold a particular set of beliefs or attitudes, he must be able to apply them, resolve conflicts between them, and form a more complex defense for his actions.

Let's continue our examination of the use of force doctrine. In addition to knowing the force continuum, recruits must learn that their use of authorized force is governed by many factors — including the size and gender of the suspect, the suspect's words and actions, the weapons available, and the suspect's level of resistance. This comprehensive understanding reflects an ability to make a successful value system judgment about the use of force.

As a result, consider the following objective:

At the end of this block of instruction the student will …
    Discuss the relationship between the police officer's use of force and
        the suspect's level of resistance, in compliance with departmental
        standards. [Affective — 4]

Thus, when a student is participating in a scenario-based learning (SBL) environment, he can articulate his reasons for using force in a way that is compliant with the force continuum, taking into account the various factors involved in assessing threat levels and acting accordingly. This type of objective assesses the organizational ability of the student to know and understand values and demonstrate a complex awareness of the interplay between conflicting models.

Affective Level Five: Characterizing Data or Values

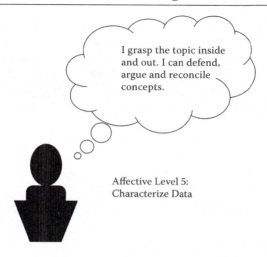

I grasp the topic inside and out. I can defend, argue and reconcile concepts.

Affective Level 5:
Characterize Data

At the end of this block of instruction the student will ...

Complete an after-action review of a subordinate officer's actions following a critical use of force incident, encompassing the following factors: degree of officer's compliance with departmental standards, officer level of force, available weapons, suspect's level of resistance, and mitigating environmental circumstances. [Affective — 5]

Compare the contents of this objective with those we have previously studied. This is a significant departure, at the highest level of training, from mere appreciation or awareness to deep, thoughtful comprehension. This objective clearly outlines the expectation that the student is to have *full mastery* of the topic.

What does it mean to be able to characterize information? This quality enables the student to determine whether information is important and to what degree it is important. As a case in point, consider this example. In the 1990s, Senior Corporal Gary Croxdale of the Dallas Police Department taught police recruits about one sign of potential aggression in suspects that he had observed, researched thoroughly, and documented through dash-cam video evidence. It was a small, inconsequential movement, but it had incredible consequences for the officers who were not aware of the significance. We watched video after video of traffic stops and field interviews, distinguished by this one small, seemingly insignificant gesture of the suspect. After the suspects demonstrated the gesture, within seconds, the officers were attacked, resisted, shot, or killed. What was this gesture? Prior to the first strike, all of the suspects reached up with one hand and smoothed their hair from back to front.

Croxdale pointed out that his anthropology-based research indicated it was a primitive behavior, also seen in primates like gorillas and apes. He believed that this subconscious, hair stroke was designed to either "psyche up" the offender for attack or a last-ditch effort to calm down escalating adrenaline levels. Whatever its origin, "going to the hair" was an unconscious telegraphing of emotion that provided a significant edge to officers who, once they were taught to see it, could *characterize* the significance of this suspect behavior.* Thus, having the awareness to not just notice the behavior but to understand the connotations is a level five skill.

It is important to recognize that being qualified to characterize information is the highest level of affective learning. Thus, if a student is capable of characterization, he is probably on his way to becoming an expert in the topic.

Final Commentary on Affective Skills Training

Police officers want to become experts in topics of interest, whether it is firearms, officer survival, or accident reconstruction. Objectives that allow officers to demonstrate a thorough understanding, coupled with their own highly developed opinions, provide a framework for a stimulating classroom experience.

Affective objectives present the most important opportunities for improvement of the existing criminal justice curriculum in most police academies. Cultivating a mere awareness within the student of contemporary issues in policing and challenging students to see the conflicts between competing values is an affective process, and a highly valuable one. However, to be able to equip the students with the tools to resolve those issues through careful analysis, organization, and value judgment is a truly important and groundbreaking endeavor.

Passion in the classroom begins and ends with targeted affective training objectives. After all, the difference between a great teacher and an extraordinary teacher is this: Great teachers know how to inspire passion in their students within narrow areas of expertise. Extraordinary teachers set the hearts of their students afire with zeal for the topic, and they can do it with *any* topic because they understand that students want to be affected by what

---

* During my years of street patrol, I noted this suspect movement on many occasions, especially among mentally fragile offenders. It was almost always an accurate predictor of resistance by the suspect, and it was something I taught to hundreds of recruits over the years. I owe Gary a great debt of gratitude for this crucial observation that has saved lives.

they learn. Affective training inspires, inflames, and inculcates deep awareness and belief systems that can make classroom training for police officers
a more dynamic process. Use affective training objectives wisely to renovate
existing programs and measure the results for yourself.

Five Levels of Ability
Police Psychomotor Skills Training

8

There were hundreds of times in my career when life-and-death decisions had to be made. I made many of them "from the gut" and regretted very few.

—Richard Marcinko

Psychomotor skills make up many of the competencies that police officers need on a day-to-day basis. For example, driving, shooting, and fitness skills are required psychomotor components of police academy training. Psychomotor objectives aim to pair the mind ("psych") with the body ("motor") successfully, culminating in an expected level of student performance that meets certain defined standards.

Psychomotor training is, by and large, well developed in the police profession. Our defensive tactics, firearms, and emergency vehicle operations are among the best training programs that police academies have to offer. The reason for this is simple: When learning psychomotor skills, you can either demonstrate the skill or you cannot. There is no intellectual defense or internal emotional process for the instructor to gauge. Can the student successfully navigate the obstacle course or not? Is the student able to drag a 150-pound dummy twenty yards in thirty seconds or not?

The quality of any psychomotor training program is almost entirely distinguished by two factors. The first is instructor technical expertise. Instructors who are practiced authorities on their respective skills are not difficult to find. Experienced administrators look beyond mere certifications, however, and must consider the willingness of candidates to learn how to become excellent teachers as well as practitioners.

One of the most common mistakes in selecting new training staff is the reliance on paper accomplishments as a substitute for training skill. Consider that the most important competency of trainers is not their ability to do the skills themselves but their ability to transmit their knowledge of those skills to others. Akin to coaching in professional sports, psychomotor trainers must be able to motivate, instruct, and correct students in technique. Assessing potential instructors in terms of their ability to communicate is tremendously vital. Some programs, including many in the college setting, ask instructor candidates to prepare a fifteen-minute instructional block on a topic of their choosing. This block is presented to a group of experienced instructors as part of the interview process, allowing the existing staff to determine their level of expertise in communicating concepts.

The second factor that directly impacts the quality of psychomotor programs is the accessibility of high-quality equipment and/or facilities. Without the proper tools, it is difficult to do an outstanding job. This is not to say that improvised materials and settings are not adequate. In fact, inventive solutions can result in a superior training environment. In one instance, a skills trainer in the Northeast negotiated the use of an empty historic building adjacent to the police academy for recruit tactical training, without cost; they agreed to clean up the debris inside and maintain a locked building when it was not in use. A large urban department in the South approached an industrial business park complex to partner with them in executing a recruit night patrol training exercise quarterly. The agreement allowed the department to have the use of multiple offices and warehouses for building searches from 10 P.M. to 2 A.M., when the businesses were closed. The business owners were pleased to assist the police department and at no cost to the parties involved.

Technology continues to provide police departments with opportunities to acquire new gadgets, sometimes at considerable cost. New equipment is not always affordable, especially for smaller departments. Agencies with limited funds can still use older equipment to accomplish the same psychomotor goals. One branch office of a federal law enforcement agency acquired a fifteen-year-old FATS® system (Firearms Training Systems, Georgia) for no cost when a local department moved to implement Simunitions® (a subsidiary of General Dynamics, Quebec) training. The older FATS® system was no longer cutting-edge, but the shoot–don't shoot scenario capability it provided allowed the training staff to reinforce a timeless law enforcement dilemma in training their agents.

Let's conduct a brief overview and explanation of the various levels of performance within the psychomotor domain to further understand what distinguishes novice level training from expert level performance.

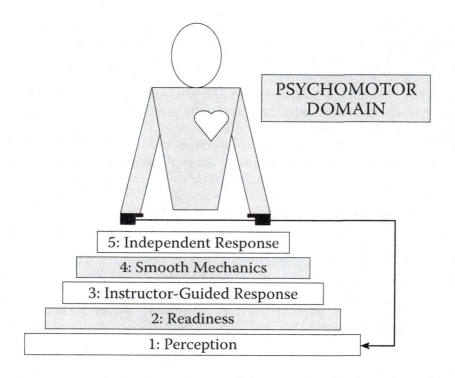

Psychomotor Level One: Perception of Need for Action

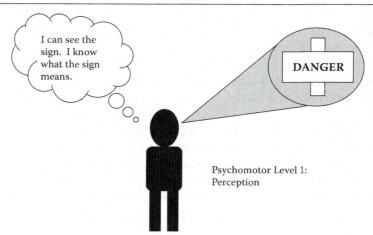

Recall that the majority of police recruits entering the profession have never been involved in any kind of physical confrontation.* Though police offi-

---

* See author's note on intake study in Chapter 7: Affective Level Two.

cers are no longer the ill-regarded brutes of the last century, the potential for use of force on street patrol is very real. Regardless of gender, stature, or experience level, police officers must be ready to take charge and, occasionally, execute violent action in a law enforcement capacity.

Over the course of years, experienced police officers have seen a variety of situations. We have learned that family members will call the police on their brothers, mothers, and children and then physically fight with the officer who is trying to remove the suspect from the home. We begin to take notice of the shifting body positions, hands in the pockets, and the furtive glances toward the alleyways when interviewing a suspect. We have seen hardened offenders say, "I'm not going back to jail," before they attack us and our colleagues. How do we prepare recruits who have no frame of reference for this kind of eventuality? The answer is, at the lowest level, development of the ability to perceive the need for action.

Consider the following objective:

At the end of this block of instruction the student will ...
    Recognize the physical signs of imminent suspect resistance.
    [Psychomotor — 1]

This kind of training is the cultivation of the awareness of the "hair on the back of the neck" phenomenon, known to soldiers and police officers alike. Richard Marcinko, the retired commander of the U.S. Navy's SEAL Team Six, writes in depth about his deep respect for this innate survival instinct in his *Rogue Warrior* books on unconventional warfare. He credits this subconscious reckoning of danger with saving his life on multiple occasions while at war in Vietnam and beyond.

Let's examine a police-oriented example. One police-involved shooting I responded to involved an officer working an off-duty job in the lobby of a hotel. This hotel was not upscale but had been the scene of a recent armed robbery. By his own account, Officer Lyle* was sitting complacently in the empty lobby, when he decided to go out to his vehicle to fetch a magazine to read. While Lyle was in his darkened car, he saw an older Buick pull up to the front of the hotel fifty yards away. He noticed it because it was his job to do so but dismissed it as a safety concern almost immediately. Probably just guests checking in to the hotel, he thought. When he exited his vehicle to return to the lobby with the magazine in hand, however, Lyle felt an inexplicable, uneasy sensation of *the hair on the back of his neck standing up* when he looked at the idling Buick, empty of passengers, in front of the hotel. When he entered the lobby, he walked in on an armed, hooded

* Fictionalized name.

assailant robbing the business. The assailant turned toward him with the gun. Lyle immediately drew his weapon and fired, critically injuring the suspect and saving his own life. His survival instinct, literally the hair on the back of his neck, allowed him to survive this incident.

Teaching recruits an awareness of their own survival instincts can be a difficult process. Exposing them to mock situations involving suspense and danger can be highly effective for some recruits. However, other recruits will not respond physiologically to scenario-based learning (SBL) situations that are obviously not real.*

Instead, consider this objective:

> At the end of this block of instruction the student will ...
>> Recognize the physiological signs of imminent, combat-induced officer exhaustion. [Psychomotor — 1]

One outstanding defensive tactics instructor named Rick Harding implemented this objective in week two of recruit physical training. He called this exercise "Running the Gauntlet." Whereas one approach might have been to develop a PowerPoint presentation about the biological basis for muscle fatigue and exhaustion and present this to a class of recruits, Rick preferred a more dynamic method of instruction. Recruits entered the mat to traverse six thirty-second rotating stations: punches, kicks, elbow strikes, knee strikes, wrestling, and grappling. They remained in the gauntlet until they recognized the signs of their own imminent physical exhaustion. This is a classic level one psychomotor exercise.

Indeed, officers who have survived in lethal encounters have supported the use of this kind of exercise. These officers articulated that they physically fought with subjects who were high on drugs or exhibiting excited delirium, who were nonresponsive to impact and chemical weapons. They were reluctant to use their firearm until they began to realize that they themselves were becoming irreversibly fatigued. Officer Diggs† fought with a mentally ill subject for four full minutes, caught on his in-vehicle camera, before resorting to the use of his firearm:

> ... I could feel myself getting ready to black out. Nothing was working — control moves, baton, pepper spray. We were both sweaty and he was still fighting like he would never quit. I realized I was going to lose the fight if I didn't do something quick. ...

---

* Young people who have spent the majority of their formative years engaged in realistic game-playing often have suppressed emotional responses to perception of danger.
† Fictionalized name.

Level one psychomotor training introduces recruits to awareness of danger not just in confrontational settings but in driving and shooting scenarios as well. Becoming acquainted with the feel of a police vehicle in an uncontrolled skid and recognizing the need for corrective steering is a fundamental emergency vehicle operations skill. Likewise, developing attentiveness to a firearm malfunction simulated with a dummy round load and the tap-rack-bang clearing action is an excellent perception-level exercise.

The key aspect of level one psychomotor objectives is the development of perception. Viewing videos that reinforce the "need for action" mantra can be of significant value when teaching at level one. Play a police incident on film, stopping it periodically to ask students, What do you see happening here? Point out body position, signs of escalating aggression, and the language that is used. Allowing students to critique fellow officers' positions during a field interview, noting whether a suspect's behavior is risky and the like are most beneficial in establishing level one skills.

Psychomotor Level Two: Ready for Action

Psychomotor Level 2: Ready for Action

Understand that the recruit's skilled execution, a requisite for higher levels, grows first out of fundamental recognition of the need to take action. Once we have established a level of perception in the student, we must then ingrain the readiness to act. We prepare our students in readiness skills by teaching them the proper stance, the equipment placement on the duty belt, and how to access the tools of the trade rapidly and decisively, when needed. It is the development of this skill, *readiness*, which differentiates police officers from civilians. This accomplishment, the cultivation of readiness, causes the humble beginnings of the emergence of the so-called police personality.

Certainly, other factors play a role in transforming young police officers from pantywaist, hand-wringing civilians into brave, albeit detached crime-fighters. Becoming emotionally and physically prepared for navigating dangerous circumstances, like war or street patrol, is a transformational experience. The world becomes a brutal place for the new police officer who sees the reality of his first homicide scene, the face of an abused child, or the elegant somberness of a police funeral. Emotional readiness prepares students for a long career in the trenches of street work. In the development of physical readiness, however, the recruit takes his first steps toward establishing the identity he needs for success in the profession. As trainers, we must carefully recall that transformational process from our own early days in the field and work to instill the physical capability for ready action in our students.

Consider this objective:

At the end of this block of instruction the student will ...
During a mock field interview, demonstrate a safe stance.

Is this objective complete? No. This objective fails to tell us what constitutes the definition of *safe*. It is a shaky premise to assume that all instructors will be able to judge what is safe and what is not, over the course of time. What is needed is a more defined version of the above objective, complete with information about what is specifically required of the student. Let's consider the following revision:

At the end of this block of instruction the student will ...
During a mock field interview, demonstrate a safe stance incorporating the following qualities: maintain a distance of four or more feet from the subject, displaying a bladed body position with weapon side to rear, with hands in a neutral, ready position. [Psychomotor — 2]

This objective details the expectations of safe in a way that there can be no mistake. In turn, this mirrors the reality of the job of police work in a much more true fashion, does it not?

Psychomotor Level Three: Guided Action

Psychomotor Level 3:
Guided Action

Guided action is the intermediary step between learning a new skill and mastering it. What is important about level three training is the *direction of the instructor*. Without existing skills in an area, students will need to practice new skills under the careful supervision of an instructor. An easy illustration of this level in action is this: Imagine a class on basic handcuffing skills. First, the students will watch the instructor apply the handcuffs to a subject. Next, the students will try to imitate what the instructor did. This is the "do–show" method used for level three objectives: The instructor will do it and then the students will show it.

Thus, consider:

At the end of this block of instruction the student will …
At the direction of the instructor, demonstrate the steps in applying
handcuffs to a prone and compliant subject. [Psychomotor — 3]

The student is not expected to know when or why to put on handcuffs — that decision-making ability is a cognitive, or perhaps even affective, skill. The psychomotor skill is the execution of the physical action and, at level three, it is action at the direction of the instructor who guides and supports the student who is learning the skill. Training at this level is like making a parachute jump *in tandem* with your teacher. The teacher is in control but allows the student to do what he is capable of doing, perhaps pulling the chute cord or steering, with the help of the instructor.

Psychomotor Level Four: Habit of Action

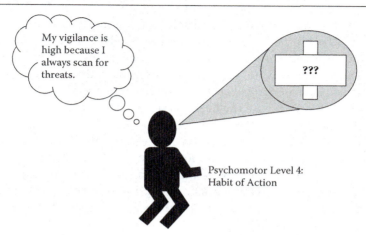

My vigilance is high because I always scan for threats.

???

Psychomotor Level 4: Habit of Action

As instructors, we must devote ourselves to the establishment of officer survival habits in our students. Obviously, the most important habits are those that will keep officers from harm, but habits extend beyond these topics. Habits of action in completing paperwork well, conducting field sobriety testing, and testifying in court are also crucial to good police work. Excellent field trainers teach their rookies to always do things the same way, each and every time. Habits of action become fluid, especially under duress.

As a rookie policeman, Officer Lyle was involved in a police shooting at the scene of an off-duty job at a hotel. His training had prepared him for this experience by driving home one exceptionally important, universal law enforcement maxim during his time in the academy. In the halls of his academy, recruits were regularly disciplined for keeping equipment in their weapon-side hand. Officer Lyle recalled being punished twice for this "offense" in one week. His instructors repeatedly said: Don't ever carry anything — not your paperwork, flashlight, or satchel — in your gun hand. One the night of his police-involved shooting, he had rolled up and placed a paper magazine in his back pocket before entering the lobby where the shooting occurred, leaving his hands ready for action. Why did Officer Lyle do this? His answer: *out of habit*. In fact, this habit may have saved his life that night.*

Firearms instructors at the Federal Law Enforcement Training Center had their hands full after the events of 9/11. When I traveled to Artesia, New

* By his own admission, Officer Lyle did not have the habit of wearing his body armor at his off-duty jobs or even during regular patrol shifts. He had failed to wear his vest on this particular night because of the summer heat. Since this event, he developed a new habit of wearing it, regardless of the weather.

Mexico, to begin my training as a Federal Air Marshal, I was a mediocre marksman. As a recruit in the police academy, I had quarreled with the fire-arms instructor who wanted to transition me from the Sig Sauer P226 to the P225, the "little brother" version for smaller hands. I won that battle and kept the big gun, but without the practice I needed, my scores were merely passing. During the Air Marshal firearms training course, we students had the opportunity to have truly world-class instruction and virtually unlimited rounds for practice. Because the firearms skills were so critically important, we practiced for hours each day on reloads, failure drills, and speed drills. Over time I realized this: When I drew my weapon very fast, I was off the mark on the target; when I drew smoothly, I was able to hit the target every time. The instructor, a former Navy SEAL, placed his hand on my shoulder and spoke the truest words in marksmanship I have ever heard: "Smooth is fast." The important concept is that speed is not the best measure of success — it is smoothness, due to habit.

> At the end of this block of instruction the student will …
>> During a response to a mock call for service, approach the scene in a tactically sound manner, encompassing the following: con-firming arrival with the dispatcher, exiting the vehicle immedi-ately, and using caution when making contact with role players. [Psychomotor — 4]

Habits are inculcated over hours of practice and training to establish *muscle memory*. This muscle memory creates an automatic response in the student, when the response is needed quickly. Imagine a young child first learning to catch a ball. Initially, the ball bounces off his inert, outstretched hands. Next, the child moves too slowly to react to the ball's approach. Lastly, the child learns to gauge the approaching ball's arrival and respond with his hand movement to catch it.

When conducting SBL exercises, instructors often expect to see habits of action in students who have not had the opportunity to practice the skills. It is important to realize that habits cannot be developed without practice. Repetitions are needed to reinforce habits — many more repetitions than are currently given in most police academies.

With the exception of firearms training, emergency vehicle operations, and some defensive tactics programs, very little time is devoted to the estab-lishment of habits in police training programs. Police recruits need to prac-tice simple competencies like approaching a call for service; standing and interviewing victims, witnesses, and suspects in a safe manner; and taking note of potential cues of violence. When asked, recruits will always indicate a preference for practicing these skills rather than hearing about them in a classroom setting.

Psychomotor Level Five: Independent Action

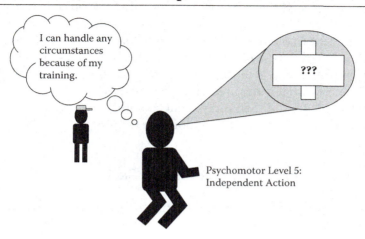

I can handle any circumstances because of my training.

???

Psychomotor Level 5:
Independent Action

At the end of this block of instruction the student will ...

> During a mock arrest scenario, given a subject who resists arrest, exe-
> cute a lateral vascular neck restraint (LVNR), strikes to green or
> yellow zones, or apply alternative hard empty-hand use-of-force
> techniques, in accordance with departmental policies, until the
> subject complies with the student's verbal commands.

Within this objective, take notice that the student has some latitude to operate. He may decide to apply the LVNR, strikes, or other methods to meet the
expectations of the course objective. At times, it is important to limit the student's choices. For example, if we do not specify a level of force, a student may
decide to flee the room and call for backup, avoiding the danger inherent in
the scenario design. Notice that the student is restricted to hard empty-hand
techniques — no batons, chemical spray, or firearms can be used to meet this
objective. Thus, in preparing the student for testing in this objective, it would
be important to remove the student's duty belt, thereby removing the tools
that are not allowed.

Another way to think about the concept of independency and competent
action is to consider the martial arts. Martial artists are expected to participate
in one-on-one competitions with other students to demonstrate their level of
understanding of the fighting concepts within their school. Within the psychomotor domain framework, martial artist competitions would mark the highest
level of response and ability because they require the student to demonstrate a
complex, independent response to a challenger. Does anyone recall the pivotal
scene in *The Karate Kid*, where the hero, Daniel-san, looks to Mr. Miyagi on
the sidelines for guidance on how to beat his opponent using the ignominious

Crane kick? Although he was proclaimed a champion, Daniel was operating at a much lower level than that of a master. Level five objectives require the student to resolve the problem on his own, *independently* of instructor assistance. A student who requires intervention by his teacher, coach, or sensei is not qualified to pass these objectives, because he cannot do so without help.

The emphasis here is on truly independent action — the ability of the student to know what is required, have the intrinsic muscle memory to execute the technique, and then carry it out smoothly, without assistance. This capability is the highest level of psychomotor training.

Final Commentary on Psychomotor Skills

Psychomotor programs, as they exist currently, are outstanding in many law enforcement training venues. If improvements are needed, it may be a matter of need for greater instructor expertise, creative engineering of venues or materials, or newer equipment. A crucial need is in the development of realistic psychomotor objectives for law enforcement officers. Solid psychomotor skills, particularly those requiring a level of fitness, are certainly needed by police officers in contemporary society.

Aside from fitness-oriented training, the development of realistic objectives based on a task analysis is the best preparation for high-quality training. Police officers in the field can provide the most information about the kinds of physical activities they perform on a regular basis. For example, as a rookie officer in an urban setting, one skill I needed in the first year of patrol work was the ability to kick in a locked apartment door. However, I had no information about technique or training in how to do this and, consequently, relied on more experienced officers when the situations arose requiring this skill.

Psychomotor training objectives are the most important objectives in police training programs. Examine the programs under your purview for relevance, challenge, and complexity. Remember that police recruits who graduate from the academy will be operating in complex, dynamic environments requiring split-second decisions. The vast majority of these decisions will be made alone, while operating in a one-man unit on the mean streets. We instructors owe these students a fighting chance in these situations. We can meet our obligations to these students by providing realistic training and encouraging the development of scenario-based environments that allow students the latitude to decide on a course of action to demonstrate their skills in a controlled environment.

Basic Instructional Methodology for Law Enforcement Training

9

Before I came here, I was confused about this subject. Having listened to your lecture, I am still confused. But on a higher level.

—Enrico Fermi

Imagine that you have been selected to attend a week-long class entitled Advanced Tactical Firearms Course. The class is being held at a $5 million training facility, complete with classrooms, an indoor shooting range, and a "Hogan's Alley" style shoot-house. The class description invites participants to bring a range of weaponry, including submachine guns, rifles, semiautomatic pistols, revolvers, and shotguns, on the first day of class. You gather your equipment, stow it in your gear bags, and report for the class, perhaps even feeling optimistic about the learning experience ahead.

You arrive at the facility and approach the building. A horde of wrinkled schoolmarms approach, canes in hand. They remove your equipment and store it in large metal lockers, securing them with combination locks. Then, they lead you to the classrooms, where you sit in assigned seats. The walls are a dull green, and a chalkboard is covered with information for you to copy. Here is where you will spend the next week. No gum chewing or drinks are allowed. They gleefully inform you that there will be a test at the end of the week to make sure you have been listening.

You are painfully disappointed by the choice of the lecture-based instructional method for this topic. Why? The answer is simple: you expected more from this course. You assumed that there would be a little action involved, excitement, range time, and student participation. After all, isn't Tactical Firearms about, well, using firearms? Instead, you are subjected to hour upon hour of the instructor talking, as you sit in neat little rows, recalling the misery of your high school days. And yet, how many of our police education courses are reminiscent of high school, both in their design and results?

There is a reason that people become police officers. We do not like to sit in classrooms, listening to lectures and doing nothing all day. Recalling our discussion from Chapter 1, police officers are, by our very nature, *action-oriented* people. A lecture-based environment is the worst punishment imaginable for people like us. We would rather be in the gym trying out techniques, putting rounds down range, or navigating a scenario-based practical exercise.

Many professional trainers do not believe that there are any alternatives to the lecture and slide show. I once worked with a very experienced colleague, Kate Baldwin,* who had been developing training for a key federal law enforcement agency for twenty years. Her training program was almost exclusively conducted for local, street-level police officers and supervisors. Kate's idea of a creative instructional design was to jazz up the slide show with exciting animation. When she clicked the mouse, the next bullet point would zoom in from the left or screech in from the right. There were bouncing bubbles to circle important words on the screen and, for very exciting phrases, the words might spin around before coming to rest in a nice, color-coordinated, extremely boring series of two hundred (or more) slides. Her training was difficult for police officers to endure and utterly disastrous for the program whenever it was presented.

I approached Kate about her methods and suggested that we work on changing the focus from the slide show presentation to the motivation of the *students*. I offered that my years of experience in training police officers had taught me that they like to be engaged and active participants in the class, not passive recipients of canned information. We could design the course as an exploratory experience, where the students would seek out answers, using experience and research, to the instructor's carefully constructed questions. Using my plan, the instructor would become the *facilitator of learning*, not merely the mouthpiece for information.

Kate was a well-intentioned, highly experienced educator, but she allowed her ego to keep her from making any progress. In her world, the existing, comfortable (for her) way of teaching, using a slide show and lecture, was the best way to convey information. In the end, she continued to train police officers in her set method; the results were predictable.

A vast majority of police training programs are designed in this exact fashion: canned, dry material with little or no features of a dynamic instructional method. So many instructors have been given an existing slide show presentation and are expected to simply lecture within the gaps, hoping that the students will be able to recall the information that was presented as they sat passively, wishing they were elsewhere. The slide show is the veritable and antiquated dog-and-pony show that makes (and subsequently breaks) the instructional process in police training.

Yet, there are alternatives to this antiquated approach. For newer trainers who still experience some anxiety about teaching, these methods have the added benefit of taking the spotlight off of you, the instructor, and throwing it onto the students. This chapter explains some of the basic options besides straight lecture and slide show that are available to law enforcement trainers.

* Fictionalized name.

All of these methods have been used in law enforcement audiences nation-wide with great success. We will examine the benefits and limitations of each of the methods and examples of how they have been used by various trainers in different topics. Within each method is a specific lesson for trainers to maximize impact. The use of some or all of these methods will make class-room instruction more engaging, student oriented, and dynamic.

Ice-Breakers

The use of ice-breakers is not a new concept. The purpose of this kind of exer-cise is to promote an atmosphere of comfort, connection with others, and, perhaps, even humor. There are some occasions when you would not bother with an ice-breaker — a short two-hour class, for example. In circumstances where you will have a group (sometimes called a cohort) of people together for any longer than a single day, it is best to instill a basic level of team-building. Whether you call it unit integrity or simply group identity, the idea is to facil-itate relationships, increase the interest of the participants in one another's ideas and language, and, of course, simple student participation.

Setting the tone very early in the class with a short exercise that conveys the fact that you (the instructor) will be including the students in activities will, likewise, increase interest in *your* classroom presentation and respect from the participants. It is a little like the idea of "You scratch my back, I'll scratch yours." When law enforcement students believe that you, the instruc-tor, are interested in what *they* have to say, they will be more interested in what *you* have to say.

You might be asking yourself, Why should I waste time with a silly ice-breaker before getting down to business? The answer is because your stu-dents want you to. Police officers are notoriously uncomfortable in the class-room. They arrive early, pick a seat in the back of the room so they can watch the entire area, bringing a folded newspaper and industrial-sized coffee cup, and plan on a long, boring stay in your class. Ice-breakers do two things to defeat this carefully crafted shelter-in-place classroom strategy of police offi-cers. First, they allow (and, with police audiences, the more accurate descrip-tion is *force*) participants to get involved. Once students get involved, they are *invested* in the outcome. They begin to take responsibility for the results because they are now actively involved in what is happening. This process taps into the very personality of police officers — the desire for control of cir-cumstances and recognition as competent, confident people. Despite them-selves, they begin to care about what it being taught.

Second, ice-breakers bring humor into the entire training process. Although we have some truly brilliant people in this profession, many police officers do not have positive memories of the educational system. The mere idea of attending a class can induce the latter group to feel miserable, anxious, or frustrated. However, a universal quality in police officers is the capacity for humor, especially dark humor, a sarcastic and cynical wit that can chide both friends and enemies alike. Cops can recognize one another by the humor that they use. In the classroom, use this to your advantage. Construct an ice-breaker that allows the introduction of humor and watch what happens.

Ice-breakers can be conducted orally, via written materials, or by more creative methods. Some exercises I have seen have been fantastic and well received by police audiences; others, not so much. One exercise I have seen involved the students drawing pictures: self-portraits, that of a police officer, their favorite firearm, etc. Another exercise required students to speak for sixty seconds on a random topic such as "Old King Cole," "chaps," or "origami." Certainly, it is possible to find an infinite variety of ice-breakers in excellent books or via the Internet. Some of the best exercises are designed by creative instructors themselves, who have a good sense of what kinds of ideas would be interesting to the police audience.

The best success I have seen with the use of ice-breakers in law enforcement training has been the "Two Truths and a Lie" exercise.* This ice-breaker is best conducted with no more than twenty-five students. Students are given a blank three-by-five index card and the following instructions:

> On your three-by-five card, write three statements about yourself. Two will be true statements and one will be a lie. Make the lie difficult to guess; for example:
> I was born in Germany.
> I was involved in a serious motorcycle accident when I was nineteen years old.
> I have five children.
> In just a few moments, you will read your statements and your peers will try to guess which statement is the lie. Your peers are allowed to ask you a few questions about your statements to try to find out which statement is the lie. Be prepared to bluff your way through this short interrogation. Good luck!

The instructor then gets the group started by going first, reading his or her three statements. Initially, the instructor should model the kinds of questions that can be posed to the next several players. Once the exercise gets going, the students will take over the interrogations with enthusiasm.

---

* There are a number of different sources for this exercise, both in print and online; thus, I cannot cite a definitive single author. Thus, understand that this exercise is not of my own design; I merely have adapted it here for the purpose of illustration.

Why does this exercise work well with the police audience? The answer is because distinguishing truth from lies is a common activity for police officers to perform. Police officers are interested in learning how to detect deception. This brief activity is well matched to their skill. Plus, it is fun to grill your cohorts. It also preserves discretion. Players do not have to reveal any more detail about their personal lives or abilities than they wish to, unlike drawing or expository speaking activities.

Although an ice-breaker is not always recommended, it can be a high-light of the day for students who dislike the classroom intensely, as many police officers do. It is best to use them in small classes, when you have at least one full day with the students.

Brainstorming

The concept of brainstorming is another simple instructional design con-cept. Ask participants to throw out any and all answers to the instructor's question. Brainstorming is an especially good way to begin a class. It demon-strates that the instructor will be inviting student interaction and creating a positive environment for active learning.

If we want students to learn in our classroom, we must support, even reward, responses. I know some instructors who carry a bag of candy bars into the room and toss out tangible rewards to participants. I am a fan of this approach, but I know one that is even more effective: positive reinforcement. If you want police officers to participate in your class, you are asking them to give you some things that are most important and precious to them — their opinions and trust. This is not an easy task, especially for law enforcement professionals. We prefer to stay self-contained, emotionally detached, and comfortably safe from intrusion into our personal space — physically and mentally. Thus, to overcome this obstacle, we need more than chocolate.

Positive reinforcement gives students an affirmation of themselves as important, useful members of a team. How is it done? The answer: through your commitment to positive communication with all students who partici-pate, even if you disagree with their answers.

Let's look at an example of a brainstorming question that my good friend, a police fitness instructor, posed during the first week of recruit training:

Can anyone tell me what kind of exercises will keep a police officer fit?

Initially, there may be the sound of silence when an instructor begins a class in this manner. Students will assume that this is a rhetorical question requir-ing no response *or* they will assume that whatever answer they give, it will be shot down by the instructor. In an unfamiliar classroom with an unproven instructor, students operate according to the definition of "cannon fodder." They want to know what will happen to the first student who steps on an instructional land mine: will he be sacrificed or saved by the instructor? Wait for a response; someone in the class wants to answer the question or provide an opinion. If this fails, politely require a response from one particular student and then ask: "Who else has an opinion?" Others will follow.

- Good answers.
  - Using our fitness topic example, some students may give correct answers such as "sit-ups," "running," or "weight-lifting." For these good answers, build on them and be effusive in your praise:
    - "Exactly right. _____ is an excellent answer because..."
    - "_____ has a good answer. Who else can think of one?"
- Middle-of-the-road answers.
  - For middle-of-the-road answers, praise the student for responding and redirect to the class for additional responses:
    - "That's an interesting possibility. Can anyone think of another?"
    - "_____ is on the right track. Who can help him out?"
- Incorrect answers.
  - What if a student gives a truly bone-headed response to our question? As instructors, we must walk the line between rewarding the student and ridiculing him or her. You need to respond directly without giving your own opinion or the "right" answer. Here are some phrases that might come in handy:
    - "That's one suggestion."
    - "Can you tell me a little more about that?"
    - "_____ has an interesting point of view. Who has another perspective?"

Develop questions that can generate a number of answers from students — some right, some middle-of-the-road, and some wrong. Here are some other examples of good brainstorming questions to open up an instructional block on other topics:

- Report Writing: "What kind of information do I need to write a police report?"
- Discrimination: "Some people believe that women should not be allowed to become police officers. Who can give me a reason why?"
- Use of Force: "What can a police officer do when a subject resists arrest?"

- Tactics: "What kinds of things are important to consider before making a forced entry into a residence?
- Communications: "What kind of body language indicates a person is not interested in talking to the police?"

Brainstorming sets the tone for two-way communication in the classroom and opens the door to students with existing knowledge to contribute to the class. Moreover, it provides an opportunity to build *rapport* with students. Using this technique to build rapport will allow you to generate trust and interest in whatever topic you are teaching. Also, brainstorming will draw out the key concepts that may be germane to the topic of the class. When the students can give you the opening concepts through a brainstorming activity, it reduces the need for you to lecture.

Brainstorming is a "double-dip" technique. It allows you to reach the *auditory* learners, through the spoken word and the conversation that takes place. You can double your efficiency by writing the answers that are given on the chalkboard or whiteboard to reach your *visual* learners, who need to see the information. Better yet, you can even ask for a volunteer from the class — one of the *kinesthetic* learners, who learns by doing — to write the answers for you.

Case Study/Critical Incident

We can all agree that law enforcement work requires a high degree of skill in a number of areas — knowledge of laws, legal procedures, and precedents; survival skills; and analytical skills to assess new situations and people. Thus, one of the best ways to continue our education after we leave the police academy is through staying current with new laws, events, and police activities. By hearing about what kinds of things are happening on the street, we can continue to be sharp contemporaries with our students. Many trainers stay informed through legal updates or subscriptions to Web-based information services on law enforcement activities nationwide, or even internationally. In fact, I have colleagues who routinely cull through hundreds of e-mails a month for new and critical information in their areas of expertise. Now, we can put that knowledge to good use in the development of case studies for your classroom.

Case studies, also called *critical incidents*, are constructed from a number of sources — internal happenings within a department, media accounts, and even personal experience. Ideally, the use of case studies as an instructional method is a threefold endeavor. First, the instructor will present a detailed account of a recent event to students who are assembled into small groups of four to six people per group. Next, the groups will then examine the information presented and determine the solution to a problem or answer questions requiring opinions. Last, the students will report their findings to the class.

The use of the case study is one of the most powerful techniques in classroom training that we have to illustrate learning points through examples. Case studies are high impact, interesting, and compelling. Often, they can be accompanied by visual aids, such as newspaper articles, photographs, or videos. Even students who do not like reading assignments will enjoy perusing the short account of a case study that is relevant and timely.

Using case studies to emphasize the relevancy of your class to the students' day-to-day work is crucial. For example, it would be difficult to find an example of a case study that would be broad enough and relevant for a class comprised of a mixed group of police chiefs, dispatchers, and patrol officers. Remember that you must teach to the level of your students and know their interests. In cases where you have a diverse audience of assignments, skill levels, and tenure, case studies may be difficult to use well. However, with homogenous audiences, like a class of patrol sergeants, police recruits, or trainers, case studies are ideal.

Let me offer an example. When I was responsible for a statewide certification program for law enforcement trainers, I had two kinds of students: police officers and correctional officers. These audiences were considered as one and the same by the civilian administrators, but, as we all know, the role of police officers and correctional officers is vastly different. The existing program reinforced tensions between the two groups because corrections officers were in the minority and felt marginalized by all the "cop-speak." Police officers in the class resented the presence of corrections officers as "non-police" personnel. My challenge was to develop a case study that would be relevant for both groups, because they trained together in the same classroom.

I asked myself: What do these groups have in common? Both groups worked with criminal populations, but that was hardly groundbreaking. What I discovered was that one of the main areas of confluence shared by police and corrections is that both groups are subject to potential prosecution under cruel and unusual punishment provisions of civil rights law, also called *color of law*, cited in 42 U.S.C. 1983. Using this knowledge, I reasoned that police and corrections might be able to work together on a case study drawing on a shared liability concern. Inspired thus, I located a Supreme Court case of interest and designed a case study to address this issue. The student handout is shown in its original form in the following section.

Case Study: *Hope v. Pelzer*

Under Chapter 42 U.S.C. 1983, a state actor is liable for violating the rights of others. Prisoners in a state prison have the right under the eighth and fourteenth amendments to be free from "cruel and unusual punishment."

In *Hope v. Pelzer*, Hope sued under Section 1983 after prison guards alleg-edly handcuffed his arms to a metal bar. His arms were cuffed above shoulder level. The guards made Hope take off his shirt and left him in the Alabama sun for seven hours. They denied him bathroom breaks, and when he asked for water, they mocked him. They then gave some water to the dogs and kicked over the water cooler.

The Alabama Department of Corrections (DOC) regulations authorize the use of the hitching post when an inmate refuses to work or is otherwise dis-ruptive to a work squad. It provides that an activity log should be completed for each such inmate, detailing his responses to offers of water and bathroom breaks every fifteen minutes. Such a log was completed and maintained for Hope's previous shackling in May, but the record contained no such log for the seven-hour shackling in June and the record indicated that the periodic offers required by the regulation were not made.

After assembling the students into a group and reading the facts of the case to them, I made the following assignment:

Your group has been appointed to the prison's disciplinary advisory board hearing the case of Pelzer and his fellow guards. You have 30 minutes to dis-cuss the case and answer the following questions within your group:

Were Hope's civil rights violated? Was he subjected to cruel and unusual punishment? Why or why not?

Should Pelzer and his fellow guards be disciplined for their treatment of Hope? Why or why not? What punishment, if any, should they be given?

Is Hope entitled to a monetary settlement for this incident? Why or why not? What, if any, amount would be a fair settlement to offer Hope?

What was the outcome of this exercise? The results were phenomenal. Students were energized and debated at length about the various aspects of the case. Correctional officers educated police officers about the regulations and institutional punishments that were common within their organizations. Police officers taught their corrections contemporaries about their mutual exposure under Section 1983 liability in their work on the street. Some stu-dents argued vehemently that Hope wasn't entitled to a dime in settlement because he was obviously a typical prisoner "acting a fool." Unexpectedly, others, including very conservative-minded police officers, asserted that Hope was entirely a victim of a system created to inflict cruel and unusual punishment by its very design, according to the acceptable punishments listed in the DOC regulation handbook. Students were passionately inflamed by the guards kicking over the water cooler and watering the dogs while Hope suffered in the burning sun.

What the students enjoyed about this exercise was that their role was that of the "expert." After all, they were appointed to a disciplinary advisory board — they were making important decisions of legal stature, punishment, and settlements. Thus, they were encouraged to operate at a higher cognitive level when they debated whether Hope's rights were violated and, if so, to what degree.* All things considered, this block of instruction was highly invigorating for both the students and the instructors. As a result of this success, I exported this exercise to use in my constitutional law course for police recruits with the same results.

Now, compare this approach with the old-fashioned method of reading the case aloud and pointing out to the students what the information means. In the old method, the elementary school approach, the students sit passively like sponges, presumably soaking up knowledge. In the new method, the adult learning model, the students are actively involved in the learning process. They interact with one another to learn and even debate the importance of the information. They may or may not ask questions of the instructor. This kind of experience represents a higher level of instruction than most people are used to. The results: priceless.

Case studies invite debate, challenge old assertions, and give a platform for students to truly interact with the instructor and one another in a dynamic way. Although trainers must provide guidance, they can keep their distance from the students as the students run the show and determine what is important within a case study. The small group design is a crucial component to the use of the case study and, if done correctly, can add a new dimension to your instructional ventures.

Final Commentary on Basic Instructional Methods

Trainers who are stuck in a habit of using slide shows and lecture to teach will never become excellent instructors. No matter how glitzy or sublime their slides and videos are, there is no substitute for the application of a true educator's magic. Quality educators involve their students in the learning process and engage their minds in new and interesting ways. The mastery of this skill transforms a mere lecturer into a classroom *sensei*.

The study of instructional methodology we have covered in this chapter can be easily expressed in three short phrases:

---

* Review Chapter 6: Cognitive Learning. By having students assess the level of compliance with the term cruel and unusual punishment, students were tasked with operating at level five (out of six) on the cognitive learning continuum.

Lesson #1: Break the ice.
Lesson #2: All answers are good answers.
Lesson #3: Make it relevant with quality case studies.

The lessons of this chapter are commonsense and easy to implement into existing courses with minimal time investment and skill. I recommend the use of one or all of these methods in an existing course. Try it, and ask your students for written feedback on what they thought of the exercise at the end of the course.

Intermediate Instructional Techniques

10

> When I was a fireman, I was in a lot of burning buildings. It was a great job, the only job I ever had that compares with the thrill of acting.
> —P. McGinley

On an idyllic spring day, a group of high school students sits in a class for another regular day in homeroom. The usual suspects are passing notes and laughing, doing their best to survive another boring lecture-based experience at the hands of public educators. Unexpectedly, the scythe-carrying Grim Reaper enters the classroom and points to a young girl in the third row. He calls her by name and she leaves the room with him. A police officer enters the room and reads an obituary of the girl to the class. She has been "killed" in an alcohol-related crash. Later in the day, she returns wearing a death masque of coal-black eyes and ghostly whiteface, wearing a coroner's tag. She cannot speak. That night, she doesn't return home to be with her family. She heads to an overnight retreat where she will compose an essay that begins:

Dear Mom and Dad … today, I died. I never had the chance to tell you …

That afternoon, a mock fatality accident is staged outside, complete with wrecked cars, victims in moulage, fire and police personnel, and parents of the "victims" on scene. Students who may have been laughing initially are now soberly watching the unfolding events, dramatically presented in living color with actual players. The topic is preventing alcohol-related accidents and fatalities. The program is called "Every 15 Minutes" and it was designed and developed by a police officer.

Young people are not easily affected by blood, gore, and death these days. So much carnage, both virtual and real, of murders and other events bombards us each day — whether on the news, in video games, or on the Internet. However silly or unrealistic this dramatic rendering described above may sound to us, as hardened trainers of police officers, it develops into an experience that is very real to the students it is trying to reach. "Every 15 Minutes" maximizes its impact through detailed reenactments, demonstrations, and involved role-playing.

Using dramatic techniques like those described above can be highly successful endeavors in law enforcement training, as well. Why? There are several reasons. One: it is entertaining. Two: it is unexpected. Three: Police officers are often lumped together with race car drivers and firefighters under one type of heading: so-called adrenaline junkies. Why do we seek out this profession, characterized by danger and uncertainty? The answer: because we are good at it. Skilled officers quickly learn to handle the unexpected. Like a well-played game of Texas hold 'em, you manage the hand you have been dealt; how well you play what you have is the hallmark of a professional card player. It is the same with police officers who respond to scenes unknown and manage unforeseen events as they unfold. Often this is a very dramatic experience. Bottling this experience, using drama on a microcosmic level for classroom use, can be fun, educational, and worthwhile for police training.

We know that police officers function well under stress — whether it is on the job or not. Placing law enforcement students under stress (albeit minor stress, compared with the job of patrol) challenges them to use their existing skills in new ways. Asking officers to develop a creative role-play or merely observe dynamic, choreographed action is one way to create excitement about your topic.

Instructors with a natural flair for the dramatic will add another dimension to their classroom presentation through the approaches in this chapter. Let's now explore the usage of live demonstration, role-playing, and skits in law enforcement training programs. These intermediate techniques require more skill and preparation but have memorable results in the classroom. We will examine the key properties of each technique and how to maximize their effectiveness for police audiences.

Demonstration

By now, almost every police officer in America has seen the infamous video of the ubiquitous, dread-locked federal agent who is presenting to an elementary school-aged group of children. He discusses the need for firearms safety and promptly has an accidental discharge, injuring himself, after holstering his weapon in an unsafe manner. Of course, the show doesn't end there — he continues to teach for a short time, bleeding copiously from his hip until he decides he needs to call off this particular class. A now-classic comedy of errors (but certainly not for the agent involved), this video shows how *not* to do a demonstration.

Demonstrations are designed to teach officers how to actually perform a task or skill. The concept is this: By letting students see an actual rendering of a technique or skill, students will be better able to repeat the same performance. Some of the best demonstrations are truly lively to watch. When watching a carefully orchestrated reenactment, in fact, it may be more accurate to say *experience*.

The typical demonstration that may come to mind for most instructors involves playing a video for a group of students. As technology progresses, high-quality police videos are becoming more readily available. I highly recommend using and sharing videos whenever you can. However, for the purposes of this discussion, I am referring to *live action* demonstrations, conducted by actual people, amateur actors, physically in residence in the classroom.

Demonstrations are those dramatic reenactments that are characterized by the student merely watching the action. No participation by the student is expected or desired. This passive quality does not necessarily negate the possibility that this demonstration will be dynamic or exciting, however.

Imagine sitting in a classroom where the lights have been significantly dimmed. The instructor announces that this room is now a barricaded house, a suspected drug dealer's den, and the SWAT team is about to make entry. A simulated flash-bang explodes in the room. Next, a stacked group of black-attired police shooters enters the room fluidly, moving as a unit, showing us the muzzle and flashlight discipline that make up a quality tactical room entry. Would this be an exciting demonstration to passively observe? Absolutely it would.

Contrast the above scenario with the other passive alternatives. Would you prefer a bland description of tactical entry techniques, complete with stick figure drawings on the chalkboard of positions and movement? It might make a difference if the instructor drawing on the board was an actual, bona fide SWAT team member — or perhaps not. Another choice: show a video of the technique, punctuated by loud rock music. Better, but not exactly riveting, material. No experience can compare with a live demo. Anything else is going to be less than quality.

Demonstrations require some thought and practice beforehand to achieve the best results. They are best utilized when showcasing a complex or potentially dangerous skill, like firearms techniques, defensive tactics, and emergency vehicle operations. Remember that the key aspect of demonstration, as differentiated from other dramatic techniques, is the lack of student participation as an essential element of the design. If the student participates in any way, it is not a demonstration — it is another technique.

Skits

Skits involve placing police training students in small groups and assigning them the task of creating a script *of their own design* for presentation. Most often, this might take the form of developing the "right" and "wrong" way of approaches to a problem or issue, given by the instructor. Consider, for example, that you are giving a class on interview and interrogation techniques. Your exercise might read something like this:

> Your group has been assigned to develop a skit. Select one of the following tasks for your group to showcase:
>
>   1. Conduct a field interview of a robbery victim.
>   2. Conduct a traffic stop interview.
>   3. Conduct an interrogation of a robbery suspect.

Your group will show the class two different approaches: the right and wrong ways to do this task. Use as much creativity, emotion, and dialogue as you would like. Your skit should last no longer than five minutes and all group members must participate.

The key quality of a skit, as contrasted with other techniques, is the development of an actual script. Skits should not be conducted extemporaneously, or ad libbed. Students must develop the dialogue for the presentation using their collective notes. As a result, some degree of *practice* must ensue, which allows students to move toward higher levels of learning.* Obviously, what is valuable about this exercise is the finished product — the performance that is given. However, you may consider asking students to turn in a copy of their notes for your review, depending on your particular style.

Students will surprise you with their various approaches, use of wry humor, and abject truthfulness about the underlying aspects of the assigned topic. Most importantly, students will draw upon their own experiences to create the presentation materials. This is a high-level learning activity, because it involves *synthesis* of material from wide and varied sources into a whole.† As an instructor, if you remain in the classroom during this activity, you might hear students discussing the various experiences they have actually encountered during the course of their own patrol duties, culling these experiences for dialogue and setting. The magic of this technique is that it impels learners to *teach one another* what is important about a topic.

The mainstay of teaching in the medical profession is "See one, do one, teach one." In the hospital setting, this means that a resident medical student will *see* a fellow doctor putting stitches in; next, they will *do* it themselves; last, they will *teach* another student how to do so. We can apply the same approach to law enforcement training. Using skits, students move from mere observation of a technique to teaching others what they know about a given

---

* It may be possible to classify this performance-based activity as a psychomotor level five skill, because it is characterized by independent action without assistance from the instructor.
† Synthesis is a cognitive level six activity. Review Chapter 6 for more detail on Bloom's taxonomy and classification of learning.

approach or issue. Plus, the added stress of performance anxiety can inject some life into students who would otherwise be barely awake, tapping into that hidden adrenaline junkie lurking beneath the surface of the law enforcement student.

Sometimes, these types of exercises are used nicely as a "capstone" exercise, wherein students can express their levels of comprehension of what has been presented at the end of a course of instruction. It can also work during the beginning or middle of a course to capitalize on what material has already been covered. The skit is especially effective for communication-oriented topics like interview and interrogation, tactical operations, discrimination, and radio use.

Role-Playing

As part of basic training in the southwestern United States, students often take a mandatory class in the police academy on Spanish communications. Sometimes called *survival Spanish* or *command Spanish*, police officers learn how to give orders in Spanish, understand basic questions and answers, and where to turn for assistance if they need help in the field with language. Two instructors tasked with this class may have two very different approaches. Instructor Garza,* a native Spanish-speaker, opened his class with the statistics — the numbers of Spanish-speaking people in the area — and then used rote memorization for vocabulary — listen and repeat, listen and repeat. His students did their best to remember what they could by this approach.

Instructor Contreras had a different approach. Speaking in heavily accented English, he opened his class by saying:

> Why do you recruits have to learn Spanish? Shouldn't Spanish-speaking people in this country learn to speak English instead? Let me show you why you want to learn as much Spanish as you can.

Then, he conducted a brief role-playing exercise. First, he selected a willing volunteer, who could speak no Spanish, to act as the officer. Next, he selected a fluent Spanish-speaker as the suspect. Instructor Contreras told the suspect, "Just follow my lead." He set the scene like this: the officer has arrived behind a closed business in the middle of the night. He has come upon two subjects who appear to be intoxicated in the alley. Then he said, "Officer, begin!"

What happened next was an ad lib, unstructured role-play. The officer asked the suspects what they were doing and whether they were intoxicated. Contreras and his accomplice responded, "*Como*? No English." The officer

---

* Fictionalized name.

repeated his questions and asked the suspects to turn around, keeping their hands where he could see them. Contreras turned to his accomplice and muttered:

Vamos a matar a esta puta.

His accomplice simply nodded and the officer began to approach them, repeating his commands. Contreras then stopped the role-play and asked who in the class knew what he had said to his accomplice. None knew. He asked whether his accomplice had understood. He nodded. English translation: Let's kill this bitch. The impact on the students was unforgettable. Contreras's first point of instruction followed: if you cannot speak the language, do not allow the suspects to talk with one another, under any circumstances; they might be planning to do something very unpleasant.

The powerful vehicle that Contreras gave to his instruction could have been bastardized to conform to a lecture approach. In other words, Contreras could have opened his class with a description of the event and then told students the same information. How much more dynamic was his choice of presentation? By focusing on the affective part of training, Contreras ignited a touchstone of controversy within the hearts of his students.* Students who took his class remembered, fifteen years later, that simple role-playing exercise every time they encountered a Spanish-speaking group of people. Although they may not have become fluent Spanish-speakers, they had a keener interest in learning how to speak the language than those who had not taken the class.

With a minimum of preparation, role-playing can be done on virtually any topic. What is required is an understanding of what direction you want to go with a dramatic rendering. In Contreras's case, he knew that he would mumble the crucial part to his accomplice at some point. Otherwise, the accomplice was ready to play. In other cases, there may be a need for a simple set of instructions given to your players. For example, "no physical contact" or "no profanity is allowed" might provide some guidance to unprepared, but enthusiastic, actors.

How do you design your own role-playing exercise? The answer is simple: Ask yourself what kind of situation will best illustrate your teaching point. Have you lived through a situation that can be recreated for dramatic effect? Consider, for example, teaching recruits the need to act with courtesy in dealings with the public. What can happen if an officer is not courteous? It is true that an officer can unwittingly encourage physical resistance by

---

* Understanding the value of a skill, in this case appreciation for the officer safety component associated with encountering a group of non-English-speaking suspects, is an affective level three exercise.

his actions. By treating a suspect with disrespect and challenging him with arrogance, an officer can make a bad situation much worse. You can say all of these things to a class of passive students or you can show them through dramatic role-play. Take a student out into the hall and give him a rubber knife. Tell him to stash it where he can get to it — in the small of his back or inside his waistband — and to try to use it when you use the word *pansy*. Reenter the classroom and begin by setting the stage, as Contreras did for his students. You play the part of the officious jerk cop and the suspect surprises us all when he pulls out a knife and attacks, right on cue.

Role-playing exercises provide the opportunity for spontaneous creativity, both on the part of the instructor and the students. It is participation oriented, so students can actively get involved with doing, instead of sitting. It takes less preparation than other methods and allows a wide range of activities. Caution must be advised, however, with the use of any uncontrolled action in the classroom. Overly zealous players or poor situational control can lead to physical injuries or ego bruising. Never use live weapons as a prop in the classroom — whether knives, guns, or other items. Even weapons that have reportedly been cleared and double-checked have resulted in deaths of officers in well-intentioned circumstances. Do not make this same mistake. Use training weapons — preferably the bright red kind — so there is no room for error.

Final Commentary on Dramatic Methods

If the basic methods of Chapter 9 are the band-aid approach to improving training, the intermediate methods of this chapter are the battlefield atropine injections for classes in need of true resuscitation. When executed well, these instructional methods will have a greater impact on your audiences than more basic approaches. Just a warning: These techniques are not for the shy, inhibited instructor who is uncomfortable in front of a group. They require a hands-on, inspirational type of leadership and the ability to motivate students to enter a potentially forbidding world of creative design.

Giving your students the gift of surprise is a rare and wonderful thing. The considered deployment of demonstrations, skits, and role-playing under the right circumstances can be the crucial link between the material you deliver and the material that students *remember* in the end. Under the best circumstances, especially in our profession, your inspired instruction could save a life. Dramatic techniques in the classroom are suspenseful, engaging, and memorable for students who have come to expect yet another lecture-and-slide show course. Use this fact to your advantage in the classroom and you can begin to see more dynamic results.

Construction of Law Enforcement Lesson Plans
Preliminary Development

11

> When instructors walk into a training session with nothing more than their expertise, they are practicing crisis management.
>
> —**David Torrence**

On July 19, 1989, United Airlines flight 232 was loaded with passengers and departed from Denver's Stapleton Airport headed for Chicago's O'Hare International. It would never arrive at its destination. During the course of the flight, a crucial piece of the engine disintegrated, causing a catastrophic failure of the entire plane's hydraulic system. As the pilots lost control over the aircraft's steering and speed systems, they realized that a crash was imminent. With the assistance of air traffic control, they set down on a cleared runway in Sioux City, Iowa. Erupting in a massive fireball that was caught on videotape by the local news, the DC-10 careened onto the deserted runway; 111 people lost their lives, most of them upon impact. The survivors, 185 of them, walked away from one of the worst crashes in aviation history.

After watching the video, it is incredible to imagine that such a large majority of the passengers and crew could have survived this event. The pilots credited a unique confluence of events with the high survival rate. First, a flight instructor, Dennis Fitch, was onboard the aircraft and offered his assistance to the cockpit when the engine trouble began. His skill and expertise were deemed a key factor by the National Transportation Safety Board in the successful landing of the plane. Second, the crew had recently been trained in crew resource management (CRM), which dictates that all resources — equipment, procedures, and people — available should be used in case of in-flight emergencies. CRM dictates that all crew members have important observations to make and key roles to play, especially when flight circumstances are out of the norm. This is in sharp contrast to the previously held cultural belief within the aviation community that the captain alone should be in charge under all circumstances. As a result, the pilots consulted with one another, the ground maintenance crews, and the auxiliary staff to determine what course of action would lead to the greatest chance of saving lives. Last, the ground first responder crews — firefighters, emergency medical service, and police — had an emergency operations plan that worked. The emergency plan worked because, ironically, they had practiced for just such an event. In 1987, two years before the disaster, the responder's annual training exercise focused on response to a wide-body aircraft crash at Sioux City, with 150 casualties.*

United Airlines flight 232 illustrates a classic example of successful crisis management in action. How can we apply the lessons learned from such an event to our own endeavors as instructors? Simply put, the message is clear: In order to survive any crisis, planning is essential. Certainly, an event of classroom instruction is not a crisis on the scale of a plane crash. I do not intend to downplay the significance of such an event but rather to use it as a source of inspiration for our own efforts.

In the police training realm, it is common to have an instructor who brings nothing to class but a canned slide show presentation. Is he or she prepared? No. In fact, some instructors would ask: What do I need besides a slide show? The answer: a well-developed operations plan. How do we get there? By using some of the same lessons learned in Sioux City — utilizing all possible resources, conferring with others, and practicing for all possibilities.

Thus, with this concept in mind, let us discuss some approaches to creating the fundamental plans for instruction. Instructors are the architects of the learning experience for the students. If we as instructors can liken ourselves to construction workers or foremen on a job site, think of the lesson plan as your basic building schematics. For example, there are many different designs you can use when building a house; some people prefer the saltbox, others like the colonial or rancher. Lesson plans are, once written, as individual as you are. Your lesson plan is your blueprint — it shows you where to begin digging, how the walls will go up, and so on. Can you build a house without blueprints? Yes, you can, but you probably won't want to live in it.

In this chapter, we will outline the process of beginning the development of lesson plans for law enforcement borrowing some terms from one model, instructional theory into practice (ITIP). ITIP is structure based, versatile, and easily adapted to the needs of law enforcement. There are many alternatives to this system; I have chosen it because it is the system with which I have the most skill and experience. ITIP is an approach to lesson plan development that is mainstream and accepted in the field of education, borne out of the efforts of many educational experts with a higher degree of education and a better grasp of semantics and knowledge than I can cite. I do not claim to be the resident expert in these techniques; I merely seek to acquaint the

---

* Captain Al Haynes was interviewed by the staff of NASA's Dryden Flight Research Facility in 1991. He credited the director of services, Gary Brown, with the development of this critical emergency operations plan, which called for a wide range of community-based services, across multiple jurisdictions, in Sioux City's airport emergency response.

reader with their use and to give a starting point to adapt these techniques for best practices in our field.

It is important to understand that the original lesson plan concept was developed by a traditional educator, with the plan for a more-or-less straightforward lecture in mind. Although this makes the method highly suspect for law enforcement training applications, ITIP has some distinct strong points that we can use to get our job done. Given that we want to learn how to minimize the use of lecture, we must be careful how we employ this method. After all, unwittingly becoming rigid in the approach to lesson plan development will only alienate students. Instead, the idea is to keep what is good for us and discard the rest.

In altering this method for use in law enforcement training, I need to give absolute credit where credit is due. The late Madeline Hunter, the developer of ITIP, was an enlightened and brilliant educator in her time. She worked tirelessly to improve the learning outcomes of school-aged students and inculcate new approaches to teaching skills in her sixty years of work in education. I certainly do not intend to denigrate her valuable work, in any way; in fact, I see her research as a well-constructed starting point for a law enforcement–specific take on training. Readers with further interest in the original ITIP format should research her methods themselves and draw their own conclusions about how well (or poorly) I have done her work justice in this book.

The modified ITIP structure for law enforcement training divides the lesson plan into three distinct areas: preliminary, content, and ancillary. We will define each area and how it is used. Next, we will take a closer look at each area, using examples of actual law enforcement topics, to make these concepts simpler for the reader to understand. In this chapter, we will discuss the preliminary development goals: learning how to use the anticipatory set and revisiting the subtle art of writing course objectives.

Developing Anticipatory Sets

Anticipatory means creating a sense of anticipation or excitement in your students. The anticipatory set (or A/Set) is a critical aspect of keeping students attuned to your presentation from the beginning. The first five minutes of the class is your one-and-only opportunity to engage students or shut them down. A well-constructed A/Set is the opening activity that builds interest and "buy-in" for your training session.

Do not confuse the idea of an A/Set with a mere listing of the course objectives, along the lines of "Today, we will be covering objectives A1 through A12." Under the mistaken idea that students want to hear exactly how the course objectives are written, some instructors make this announcement as part of their opening statements. Do not confuse your desire to prepare students for learning using an A/Set with this mechanistic approach.

Likewise, A/Sets are not connected with your personal greeting of the class. At this juncture, we must briefly mention the semantics of instructor self-introduction. Many otherwise skilled instructors squander the opportunity for a strong opening by instead building a detailed "hero" façade for their students. There are extensive, ego-loaded descriptions of where he has been, with whom, and what kind of recognition or awards he has received. Some instructors even create slides to accompany this personal "horn-tooting." This is a mistake with law enforcement audiences. An understated rundown of your experience is better than a blow-by-blow recounting of how many shootings (or chases, or classes) you have been involved in, because everyone in the room is the self-avowed expert at something police related. Keep your self-glorification to a maximum of sixty seconds and preferably thirty seconds or even less.

I have an excellent example to illustrate this point. In 2002, I had the privilege of attending a law enforcement training event that was conducted by experienced special operations personnel. Our instructor introduced himself simply as "Jim," with no explanation of his qualifications or background. After being put through the paces of the most challenging training I have ever had, I learned from another instructor that Jim was one of the DELTA force operators involved in the rescue of special operations forces that were shot down in a helicopter over Mogadishu (Somalia) in 1993.* It is the old saying: "Less is more." Your students will have more respect for what they hear when it is not overly grand or detailed.

To design a quality A/Set, you must consider what is interesting about your topic. One approach is the use of infamous cases. Is there a famous case that your topic can point to, as an example of what you are about to teach? For example, when I was teaching information sharing to law enforcement, I considered: What is *interesting* about the idea of information sharing? It helps catch bad guys, but *which* bad guys are interesting, dramatic illustrations of this principle in action? I decided on Ted Bundy — caught when investigators put together his travels across state lines to commit abductions, rapes, and murders — as an example of a bad guy caught through information sharing.

Likewise, I considered the fact that many arrests of notorious criminals begin as small, incidental contacts with offenders. A trooper conducts a so-called routine traffic stop and arrests Timothy McVeigh for his role in the Oklahoma City bombing. A small-town police officer in Murphy, North

---

* This event was immortalized in the book (and subsequent movie) *Black Hawk Down*. In typical fashion, our greatest heroes, like Jim, have no desire to be recognized as such. When asked, they say, "I was just doing my job."

Carolina, confronts a homeless man dumpster-diving behind a grocery store. His subject: Eric Rudolph, the abortion clinic bomber, who had a penchant for targeting first responders with secondary explosive devices.

Infamous cases have timeless appeal because most students will respond to these cases with a definitive interest in the information you are preparing to give them. Let's consider another topic. If the topic is crime scene search, for example, what cases come to mind? The O.J. Simpson case, with the infamous black glove and reportedly botched DNA evidence is one possibility. Another well-known case: the unsolved murder of Jon-Benet Ramsey, in which the Boulder police conducted a "thorough" crime scene search of the house, failing to search the basement and, unfortunately, missing the victim's body altogether? When using an infamous case, do not hesitate to show the good, the bad, and the ugly examples. Cases where key mistakes have been made often provide excellent fodder for an opening discussion.

Another approach to designing A/Sets with impact: generate skepticism or doubt in students. As a rule, when students begin to *care* about what you are about to say, they will be engaged (and presumably, awake) in your class. If you can set up students to form a strong opinion about a statement or question you have posed, you are generating "buzz" within your class. On the topic of emerging biometrics, I used this statement as an A/Set:

> I suggest to you that it is now within our grasp to never have another child abducted or murdered in the United States. With one small decision, no more children will ever be kidnapped or killed by a stranger or child molester. Would you be interested in helping to make this a reality?*

With this powerful opening statement, I developed both compelling interest and skepticism in the audience. Establishing a feeling of dissonance, or conflict, requires students to think and take a position internally. This action intentionally moves the student from passive receivers of information to active processors of data. Put simply, now they are interested. Goal accomplished.

Another approach: encouraging student participation through soliciting past experiences. Simply asking the members of a law enforcement audience:

> Has anyone here had any experience with _____? Can you tell us what happened, in sixty seconds or less?

A caveat: if you get a crummy or boring story, you only have yourself to blame, because you did ask for it. Providing a time limit up front can prevent

---

* Of course, the surprise was that the decision in question was to require mandatory microchip insertion for all citizens — an idea most controversial, especially to law enforcement.

the endless drag of a not-so-interesting story. However, when students can contribute an interesting, germane story for the class, it cements the bonds between students who are listening and the student who is speaking. In the minds of the listeners, they are pleased that one of their colleagues has some experience in the matter at hand. In the mind of the contributor, he is pleased to be heard. Also, you as the instructor have set the tone for the class as a place where student input is desired and respected. This is the kind of class that students will enjoy.

A final suggestion: tell a story. This is not a blanket invitation to start sharing your "war stories," at least not in the usual way. Learn the art of storytelling in a dramatic and interesting way. Tell the story from the student perspective — make it a journey for the student to go on.

For example, the wrong way:

> So, I was on my way to an assist officer call. Just as I arrived, the suspect shot my friend and ran toward me, so I shot him. I was nervous, but I survived.

The problem with this story is that it is all about the *instructor*. The students are a nameless, faceless audience to this storyteller, who may or may not be personally reliving this incident as he tells it. It is a highly important story, to be sure, but it is not engaging, and the students have no role in this story.

A better way is to place the listener in your shoes as you recount what happened. Tell it in present tense — it is happening here and now. Make the story come alive for the listener — it is no longer simply "your" story but a journey for the students. Now, we have the right way:

> Imagine: it is a dark and quiet night on your shift. You are parked outside a closed gas station, finishing your report when you get a call over the radio for an assist officer. You rush to the scene. Adrenaline is pumping and your mind is racing about what you will find when you arrive. You slide the car into park and get out, cautiously scanning the area. Your breath is coming quickly. A gunshot rings out, and you see your friend of fifteen years crumple to the ground, shot in the gut. A black-clad man races toward you with a smoking gun in his hand. What would you do?

This story has given the audience a role to play — each listener is the potential hero of this story, even if it happened to you long ago. They want to know what is going to happen because you have painted this story in the colors of a real experience. The audience is now living vicariously, through the storyteller. Storytelling is a marvelous technique for experienced officers who are full of war stories to share. Telling them in a dramatic, student-oriented way will change their impact, entirely.

Understand that A/Sets lay the emotional foundation for the entire instructional block you are about to present to the students. In particular, law enforcement students are already asking themselves, "Why am I here?" before the first words of the class are spoken. A well-designed A/Set answers the question of why and keeps learners motivated to hear what you have to say. Without a great A/Set as your first strike, you will be fighting a losing battle for the remainder of the day.

I used to ask my train-the-trainer students to consider the A/Set as the curiously termed *foreplay* of the class. It is the perfume on the wrist of a beautiful woman or the first spoonful of a decadent dessert that is being served. By using infamous cases (good and bad), creating skepticism, soliciting student experiences, or by sharing one of your own in a dramatic way, you can develop a starting point for a dynamic training experience. Make those opening moments the opportunity to show your best "A" game, with a solid A/Set.

Writing Valid Objectives for Law Enforcement

Recalling our discussion from Chapter 5, well-written objectives are student focused, unbiased, and measurable. They are written in terms of what is expected of the student at the end of the course. Objectives answer this one question: What will the student be able to know, say, show, or do? Most police trainers have access to courses with existing objectives. Compare whatever existing objectives you have with the questions below:

> Does each objective speak to student performance? Do they say what the student will be able to do? If yes, they are student focused. If no, they need to be rewritten with student performance in mind.
>
> Is the objective unbiased? If it contains words like *proper, to the satisfaction of the instructor,* or *correctly,* it is biased and should be rewritten with clear terms describing what is correct or proper.
>
> Is the objective measurable? If it contains phrases like *the student will understand* or *the student will know,* it cannot be measured and should be rewritten in terms of action, not reflection. The internal workings of a student's brain cannot be determined without the help of a neurosurgeon. Thus, the student must do something to demonstrate how he knows — whether it be an exam, performance-based exercise, or group activity.

Remember, objectives are the starting point for all instructional design. If you are writing a new course, carefully consider what you want the student to learn during your class before doing anything else. Have you had an amazing insight based on your recent experience with an active shooter? What lessons learned can you offer your students? What techniques or awareness can you pass on to others? This is where instruction begins, and your goals must be clear to you before beginning to develop real content.

Let's consider a class that you might develop following an active shooter takedown. You certainly want to tell your story. Taking one step beyond simply a retelling, you must dig deeper to make your experience meaningful to others. In thinking back over the experience, some lessons learned might include the need to go into a scene with determination to hunt down the suspect, the mindset needed for first responders, the need for adequate manpower/support, and the need to not become distracted by casualties in need of medical attention. Thus, you have the beginnings of course objectives:

> Objective 1: Upon arrival at the scene, appreciate the immediate need for potentially violent action, rather than perimeter security, to stop an active shooter threat.

Here, you have decided to develop the student's appreciation for the need for action — an affective objective that will change the student's feelings about this kind of situation. What kind of cases can you use to illustrate this principle in action for your A/Set? The Columbine incident (1999) and the Fort Hood active shooter (2009) are two contrasting examples that come to mind almost immediately, and for different reasons.*

> Objective 2: Recognize the four qualities of a first responder's mindset for survival of active shooter incidents.

Using this objective, you will tentatively plan to write four qualities that sum up your experiences with a personal mindset that you (or others) had that enabled you to survive this incident. This is an example of cognitive skills training — asking students to learn the four qualities. Perhaps you will need more, perhaps less, but you can start with a goal of four.

> Objective 3: Articulate the manpower requirements for active shooter incidents, based on the size of the building, geographic setting, and departmental guidelines [or book/article X].

It is important to tie your class to a form of written documentation to give your class scholarly credibility and value over time. When departmental

---

* I never like to retrospectively criticize actions taken at the scene by law enforcement, as a rule. Columbine marked a new era of evolving situations that local law enforcement was previously untrained to handle, beyond establishing a perimeter and calling in SWAT. In contrast, Fort Hood, in which a single, well-trained police officer searched for and stopped an active shooter, illustrates just how far training has come in the years since Columbine. It would be from this perspective that I would teach my class.

guidelines do not exist — for example, in smaller police departments — you might need to research to find where guidelines are in place. Educate your training directors or command staff about whatever information you uncover, referencing a larger department's guidelines, published articles, or a model standard operating procedure. Barring the existence of departmental guidelines, if you can locate a reputable reference, such as a book or article that you can use to support your training, you should mention it here, in your objective. Remember to include an accepted reference — a copy of the article or a citation of it — in your lesson plan index or appendix.

> Objective 4: During a scenario-based exercise, demonstrate the purposeful, forward action of active shooter response with regard to management of on-scene casualties seeking assistance from first responders.

Here is the opportunity to really show your creative side in the development of a structured, role-playing situation. Using this objective, you will place students in a scenario-based exercise simulating the actual conditions of an active shooter incident. Students will then show you (demonstrate) that they will not become distracted by rendering aid to civilians while engaging in a hunt for an active shooter.

Not enough classroom instruction in our profession culminates with a real experience. It is one thing to sit in a classroom and say you understand what you have passively learned — about safety, field interview, or active shooters. It is quite a different thing to be put through the emotional wringer in a practical exercise where you have to *actively* manage actors artfully concealing a weapon, running away, or injured and screaming for you to help them.* Therefore, rather than simply writing "students will understand" this concept in your objective, you will have them demonstrate the "purposeful, forward action" that you have taught within the class and defined in the objective.

With these well-rendered objectives in hand, you are now ready to begin developing content for this class.

Conclusion

Any instructional design method can be used with success to drive training sessions to a more dynamic outcome. If poorly understood, these methods can compound the problem by making a curriculum unintelligible. Many

---

* This is truly where the "rubber meets the road" for law enforcement training, and scenario-based exercises are exactly what we need more of. Coping with decision making under extreme stress is the key to surviving critical incidents, and we cannot train too much for survival.

instructors have read an existing lesson plan created by someone else, only to respond with a universal reaction: "Huh?" However, in mastering the modified ITIP as a *way of thinking differently* about training, we can make great strides in developing instruction that makes sense.

By moving away from the straight lecture-and-slide show method, these blueprints remind us to be creative when writing or revising a curriculum by focusing on different sections of the plan individually. Thus, in smaller pieces, it becomes a manageable task to answer a series of questions about each section and work on integrating different instructional methods — like case studies, discussions, and other learner-centered activities — into our overall plan.

Understanding the *process* of creative lesson plan development allows you to create seamless, engaging instruction like the great teachers do. Writing A/Sets with impact and course objectives that make sense in relation to the police officer's job are the preliminary steps in the creation of dynamic training. Emphasizing a compelling, dramatic, or charged opening to your class is the first step in seeing quality training results.

Developing
Quality Content

12

Although I am quite content with existing explosives, I feel we must not
stand in the path of improvement.

—**Winston Churchill**

During the early years of World War I, an unlikely event changed the course
of history for Germany's war machine. The Germans' ammunition and
explosive supplies were bottoming out in the ensuing months of conflict. The
Allied forces enforced a blockade on German ports, including a total restric-
tion on the import of Chilean saltpeter needed to produce ammunition. At
that time, saltpeter was the only naturally occurring element that was known
to allow the synthesis of ammonia, which, in turn, provided the base material for explosives. Under these circumstances, the Germans seemed to have
no alternatives; they would be defeated because they could not manufacture
war goods.

Then, remarkably, a German chemist named Fritz Haber and his colleagues developed a method of synthesizing ammonia in a way that was not
dependent on the crucial known ingredient at that time, saltpeter. In time,
despite Churchill's self-avowed reluctance to develop these new explosives,
the Allied forces utilized this process for our side. Fortunately, Germany
was not the victor in this conflict, despite their noteworthy technological
advancements in explosives design. And the rest is history.

Haber's groundbreaking process, although developed for the unpleasant
cause of perpetuating war, is still in use today. Haber understood the value of
the right information at the right time. He was not afraid to try a completely
new technique in the search for better results.

Chemistry versus Control

In police training, on the whole, we are often like instructors in the days
before the invention of dynamic classroom techniques. We plod along
using the time-honored techniques passed down from our forebears, the
venerable elementary school teachers and other traditional educators.
What if we could learn a new way to synthesize unlimited variety in learning experiences — a totally new approach to training that was thought

impossible before? Like Haber with his ammonia experiments, we need to work on the *chemistry* of what we do, by focusing on the content of our lesson plans.

More than simply a set of references or notes, our lesson plans should be well-written screenplays for success in the classroom. Content should be replete with opportunities to encourage interaction from and with students. It is this concept that sets dynamic training apart from mediocre instruction.

Is this too revolutionary a concept for police training? Historically, keeping students quiet has been one goal of many police educators. In many academies across the country, there is a rigid process for questioning the instructor, requiring standing at the position of attention, with a certain articulation of "sir" and "ma'am" as part of the mandatory status quo. Placing obstacles between the instructor and the student in the classroom discourages interaction and beats the students into passive submission. We want police officers who will be leaders of others, yet we treat them like second-class citizens in the classroom. Systems like these diminish the opportunity for communication and, therefore, student learning. These tired approaches, although intended to develop discipline and bearing in police recruits, have the effect of creating a highly polished apple of a student — one who looks good but has a barren, empty core.

Another approach police trainers can choose is to merely entertain students, rather than to educate them. Instructors focus on their inside jokes or YouTube video repertoire to the exclusion of content in their lessons. Actually conducting research on topics, preparing for responses to student input, and formulating quality points for debate are marginalized by these instructors. Perhaps this is the culture we want to promulgate in our training environments. Or perhaps we are ready to see an altogether new approach to an old problem.

Having considered how to begin to write an opening to your lesson plan in the last chapter, we will now move into the "meat" of course development. In this chapter, we will undertake an examination of how to develop quality content for law enforcement lesson plans. A skilled instructor insists on a quality training product. The best potential instructional product lies at the crossroads of your particular research and interests. You *can* write quality lesson plans, even if you have never attempted to do so before. If you have an interest in doing so, whether the topic is patrol related or something more creative, this chapter will help you in your efforts.

In the mission of developing your own brand of excellence as an instructor, the journey requires the divestment of your own personal ego. This does not mean that you become a wimpy grade school teacher or cater to the whims of your students in an overtly indulgent way. Instead, a dedicated instructor always takes into consideration the student's perspective of what is presented. He recognizes that, without the student, there is no class.

Well-prepared instructors work to become like hypodermic syringes — skilled injectors of needed content, saturating students with knowledge and information. Thus, as part of our examination of content development, we will review how to include checking for student comprehension at critical moments. From a student's perspective, this is the crucial link to the learning process.

Writing Quality Content

It is important to realize that there are no real shortcuts to developing quality instructional materials. Good classes cannot be begged, borrowed, or stolen from other instructors. The best instructional materials that you will ever present are developed by you. Because you will undoubtedly labor (and perhaps curse) over the process of development and the culmination of your own vision, it will be a better product.

Good content answers the following questions from the student's perspective. What *important* information am I learning? How can I *apply* this to my work (or life)?

Fundamentally, if we fail to answer both of these questions, we have failed as instructors. A student who is forced to attend a class that has no important content is not a student at all; he is simply a "body" that has been enrolled in a class that has no value. Likewise, a student who cannot *use* the information that has been taught is merely an impotent and frustrated bystander to the learning process. These students think, "Here are two (or six, or forty) hours of my life that I will not get back." And, they are right.

The foundation of good instructional content resides in answering the "what" and "how" questions. These issues should begin to become clear by simply referencing your course objectives. Remember that all of your teaching strategies should be guided by your objectives to ensure that the content does not go astray. For example, if you intend to teach a course on the Red Dog gang, you cannot allow yourself to get off-track, talking about the rival Blue Skunk (or whatever) gang. You may have some great pictures of both types of gang members, their tattoos, and activities, but you must ensure that your content is tied to your objectives to prevent the thread of information you are trying to teach from becoming lost.

This is the fundamental problem with beginning development endeavors with a slide show presentation or video and working *backwards* to write a set of objectives and content. More than any other content-related error, this particular problem is especially prevalent in law enforcement training. Verily, it has been said by others before me: Your slide show is not your lesson plan. The truly shallow effect of a slide show presentation cannot match the deep impact of quality content on students. Do not mistake your supplemental materials or visual aids for your content.

Research-Based Content

Where, then, do we begin when writing content? The answer is research. Instructors who want to develop cutting-edge courses must keep themselves current in the field. There are more places to find quality information than ever, thanks to the Internet. A variety of law enforcement Web sites offer crime reporting, opinion pieces, training advice, and equipment reviews. Legal databases offer case summaries, judicial reviews and opinions, precedent-setting legislation, and updates. Subscriptions for many police magazines are free or low cost. The conventional news media, too, offers an ever-evolving treasure trove of information for use in law enforcement training. Videos, articles, and links to other venues can be found in television- and print-based media sites, often for no cost.

Armed with the information from the past chapter and what we have thus considered in this chapter, let's look at an example of this content-building process in action. The theoretical topic: posttraumatic stress disorder (PTSD). Imagine that your police executive has tasked you with developing a two-hour course on this topic, and you must begin from scratch. First, consider how you will present your hard-hitting, controversial, or interesting A/Set. Here are the four approaches we covered, with a closer examination of the micro-processes involved in the use of each:

Approach 1: Use a notorious case.
    Is there an infamous case I can use or find on PTSD?

Media coverage of current events provides information on many potential case studies. A search for "posttraumatic + shooting" will turn up a least five separate cases. "Posttraumatic + suicide" or "posttraumatic + police" will likewise produce quite a few hits. Cull through these examples to see which case interests you.

Approach 2: Generate doubt.
    Can I make a statement that will generate student skepticism about PTSD?

Perhaps you can find a statistic about the vast (or few) numbers of true victims of this disorder. Maybe you could create a bone of contention about whether it is a "real" or "imagined" disorder. Ask yourself: What is controversial about PTSD and how can I present that controversy to the students?

Approach 3: Encourage student input.
   Can I solicit student experiences about PTSD?

Consider this question from the student's point of view. Would your students feel uncomfortable talking about their own experiences with PTSD? Perhaps they would. Law enforcement training is not known to be easily confused with attending a session of group therapy. Police officers may not want to share these kinds of experiences with others whom they do not know well. In this case, it might be better to ask whether students know "a friend or coworker" who has experienced this, to preserve the privacy of those who may not want to talk about it.

Approach 4: Employ dramatic storytelling.
   Can I share a story of my own about PTSD in a vivid, student-oriented
      way?

If you were experienced in the topic, you would need to develop an interesting way to tell the story, placing the students in the role of the hero (or victim, in this case). Personal stories are excellent, when they are told in the right way. Assuming that you have no prior knowledge of PTSD to share with students, we will discard option four.

The next step: creating objectives. You may not be able to develop any objectives until you do further research. Often, you may be handed objectives by another source, such as a curriculum development committee or supervisor. If not, you will need to write them based upon what you find in your reading and research. As you get further into the topic, your own impressions of the material will guide you toward what kinds of objectives make sense for your circumstances. For the purposes of this discussion, let's use the following objective:

Identify law enforcement work experiences associated with developing
   posttraumatic stress disorder.

Now: creating content. I recommend a straightforward approach to online research. Search online for the keywords or data that you want to use for your presentation. Once you locate some nuggets of information, cut and paste the information into a new document, and then cut and paste the Web address from the top of your screen as a link. Then, if you need to return to this site, you can do so easily. You have also begun to create a reference document for your appendix.

For users who are inexperienced in online research, let's examine this process more closely. Using a piece of blank paper, we will first create a list of all of the words here that might help us search for the information we need. We will place words in two different categories, to help us organize our thoughts: people and actions. *People* involves the kind of actors you want to read about. *Actions* refers to the types of outcome, factors, or other items that might narrow your search to the kinds of information you are looking for. Thus, your paper might look something like this example:

Keywords: Posttraumatic stress disorder, PTSD		
People	Actions	
police	treatment	suicide
first responder	attempted	murder
soldier	shot	indicted
mother	killed	children
father	stabbed	family

Using a search engine like Yahoo! or Google, you can then input your keyword and one (or more) of the people or actions from your list to find pertinent examples for review.* For example: searching for "ptsd + police + treatment" yields a number of fine results, all related to our topic. "Ptsd + father + shot" will give us other case studies that might provide interesting anecdotal information when PTSD was a factor, a father was involved, and a shooting occurred. The secret to this method is to always use the primary keyword, in a variety of combinations with other words, to find relevant hits. You will definitely have enough hits to keep you occupied, using the list above.† Try it for yourself and see what results you can find.

Documenting Research and Sources

Once you begin wading through the hits and locating information you can use, copy and paste items that are of interest into a blank Microsoft Word document titled "Research." Then, skip down a line and write "Sourced on [date] at." Copy and paste the Web address of the page you are using right below the information you have just collected. Your pasted entry might look something like this:

---

* Scores of professionals who already grasp the semantics of the basic Boolean Internet search will not be impressed by the simplified process described in this section. I include it here for users who are not experienced in using multiple keywords when researching topics online.
† There are several hundred permutations of search combinations that can be conducted from the short list we have developed here.

Police say a disgruntled man entered a clothing store on Main Street and shot his former girlfriend and her coworkers, after learning he would be fired from his job at the tire manufacturing plant. An unnamed spokesman indicated the man was treated for PTSD in 2006, after returning from a combat tour in Afghanistan.

Sourced on 11/15/2009 at www.wftv.com/article2000285-1200.html

Now, skip a few lines and continue your Net research, leaving your research document open and awaiting more entries. Copy and paste other items of interest into your research document, adding the tagline for your source below each entry with the Web address and date. Now, you can easily return to your original sources, give fair use credit where credit is due, and you don't have to print reams of paper during the research phase of content building.*

If accessible, also conduct additional paper-based research in the reading of professional journals and/or books within a library setting. If you do not have a library at your training site, an excellent place to conduct research is a local university or community college library. Do not be intimidated by your lack of recent experience within an educational setting. By and large, skilled librarians are pleased to assist scholars in their studies and enjoy finding the right materials for you. Tell them what you are looking for and they will point you in the right direction.

Remember that you are seeking a new approach to an old problem of developing quality training materials. Sometimes, that means going back to the "stacks" in search of inspiration. Photocopy pages of material that are pertinent to your research and write the name of the book and author at the top of your photocopy. Alternatively, make notes on plain paper with a tagline entry for your source just below.

Developing Teaching Points

Thus, research completed, we will begin to shape the material into lessons with a focus on pertinence for the student. This step requires organization of what information we have gathered into teaching points. Recall the two pivotal questions from a student's perspective:

What important information am I learning?
How can I apply this to my work (or life)?

---

* Consider creating a paper file of materials that are going to be used as supporting material for your presentation as an appendix to your lesson plan. In this electronic age, "going paperless" through electronic archiving is now within reach and a judicious alternative.

As you have just completed your own examination of the material, ask yourself: What information have you learned that was valuable for law enforcement? First, make a list of solid points that you think are interesting or important. In the study of posttraumatic stress disorder, for example, you will find that this malady claims civilian, soldier, and police casualties. PTSD occurs as a result of exposure to traumatic events, particularly those involving death, injury, and helplessness. It is characterized by intrusive recollection, drug and alcohol abuse, and secretive suffering. It is vastly undiagnosed and undertreated in police populations. These are crucial teaching points — important to know and interesting to hear about.

Second, beyond what is important to the topic itself, how can we teach something about this topic that is useful or applicable to the job (or life) of a police officer? This process is about ensuring student understanding. More than simply asking students if they can appreciate the relevance of a topic, this involves constructing thought-provoking questions that probe the student's developing understanding of a topic.

Staying with our topic on PTSD, we must think carefully about what kinds of questions will require insight. Then, we will place these questions into the right places, within the teaching points of our course. The traditional, pedagogical approach to this step can be summed up in this manner: "Does everyone understand what I just told you about PTSD?" We should not use this kind of question in law enforcement or any other adult-oriented classroom. Instead, we need to ask those questions that will keep the student thinking on the topic, instead of merely hearing what you have to say.

You must consider the importance and the pertinence issues in depth to arrive at the right questions to ask. In thinking about this process, one approach is to reflect on the right and the wrong of the argument. What can "go right" if the student uses what you have taught? Conversely, what can "go wrong" if the student doesn't learn what you have taught him today? Questions you might develop to pose to students might include, for example:

What kinds of things can happen if an officer has PTSD and doesn't get help?
Why would police officers care to know if they are dealing with a suspect who has been diagnosed with PTSD?

Another point for reflection is to ask how a student can use the information you will teach to make a difference, save a life, or work better, smarter, or more efficiently. In particular, police officers truly want to know what the *essential* information is that you are trying to transmit. Born out of years of interviewing people on the street, they want to know the facts, and they want them in a straightforward way. Police students want to ask their instructors: What do I need to know about this topic to use in my job? Thus, to make it relevant for police audiences, this means speaking to their immediate, job-related concerns. For example:

> How can you identify a friend or colleague who may be dealing with PTSD?
>
> What treatment options are available for police officers coping with PTSD?

These kinds of questions ask the student to live out of their imagination, actively process information, and determine solutions. You are engaging the student's brains to solve riddles, instead of asking them to listen to you solving them.

For each teaching point, develop one or two pointed questions that invite the students to think about different aspects of your topic. Pose these questions in a straightforward way and wait for a response. Build on responses you receive to invite more participation from students. This process initiates interactive, rather than passive, training.

Conclusion

The key to creating effective content begins with diligent research and ends with making the instruction relevant for the students. How? Know your audience and their mindset as police officers. Select instructional methods that require some action on the part of the student. Pose questions that touch the heart of the issue. In other words, stop lecturing and start facilitating learning. Using a modified instructional theory into a practice lesson plan will help you do these things because it forms a script for instruction. Through careful preparation of the content, the training process will unfold dramatically for you in the classroom.

The result of a passionate interest in whatever topic you plan to teach combined with a true examination of what is known — research — is how great courses are developed. A keen awareness of the need for student inclusion through thoughtful questioning is the cornerstone of quality lesson plans. This understanding, in turn, is the chemistry of dynamic content that creates excitement in the classroom.

Enhancing Instruction Approaches to Ancillary Development

13

> So I have learned to ask myself, can I hear the sounds and sense the shape of this other person's inner world?
>
> **—Carl R. Rogers**

Carl Rogers was one of the most influential psychologists of the twentieth century. His humanistic, client-centered approach to counseling changed the lives of thousands of people, including the majority of practicing psychotherapists and psychology educators. In Rogers' time, the patient was viewed as a broken, irrational creature in need of "fixing" by his or her therapist. After a lifetime of study, Rogers proposed an altogether new concept of perceiving those patients in need of help. He believed that the key to building rapport with patients was the practice of "unconditional positive regard." Simply put, the counselor would make no judgments about the inherent value of a person seeking treatment — he would treat him or her with dignity, affirmation, and support under all circumstances.

Believe it or not, this revolutionary worldview of a brilliant psychologist has direct application to our role as instructors in law enforcement. Many instructors, although well intentioned, forget that the student is the central reason for our place in the classroom. A classroom training session is not the place to seek out perpetual reinforcement of our own ideas and standing. We must put aside our inner tendency to deride the uninitiated young people we are training, whether for their lack of insight or for their level of experience, and recall why we are here. Like Rogers, we must practice the unconditional support of students in the classroom, who are seeking our counsel in understanding the concepts and practices of law enforcement.

It is true that some of the most respected police instructors are those who take a great deal of pride in their ability to control students' behavior in the classroom. Under the auspices of taking charge, they command silence, obedience, and, perhaps begrudgingly, respect. However, I suggest that the mark of a truly enlightened educator is the ability to turn over command of the learning experience to his pupils. With a wholly divested ego and an open mind, a teacher can engender the deepest level of respect from his students. It is this instructor who inspires trainees to contribute meaningful content to the class, in the form of pertinent questions, and to help his companions understand complex law enforcement concepts.

Because police students are active learners, we know that they need to learn by doing. Our profession is characterized by action, not lengthy reflection. Although some topics lend themselves easily to active methodology, it requires a more creative approach to generate active training opportunities with cerebral topics like investigative techniques, criminal law, and civil process. By learning a strategy or two that will allow students to work with materials, rather than simply hear about concepts, we can vastly increase the volume of how the content is learned and retained.

A Dual Purpose

We already know that the content of your class — the "what" of the lesson — is very important. Content based on facts and supported by research is crucial. But the most important component of content is the method — the "how" — in which you deliver it to the students. This conventional wisdom rings true in the classroom: "It's not *what* you say, but *how* you say it" that matters. Effective training culminates in the ability to successfully return to focusing on the input of the students, so they can remark and reflect on what has been learned. Thus, we move away from our scripted dialogue (the lesson plan) and into interaction with the students (learner practice and reinforcement). By embracing the practice of due positive regard, we can stimulate the exchange of insights with and between students. This methodical change to focusing on the learners' experience is the goal of the ancillary portion of training development.

In this chapter, we will explore the planning process to make this transition smooth by design. Making the transition from delivering content to asking for information about the *student's experience* of your instruction is a key competency. Rather than continually exhorting the virtues of your own internal thought process, you will turn the tables and ask the students what the lesson means to them. When planned near the end of a learning point, this method serves a dual purpose. First, you can check to ensure that learning has occurred. Consider, for example, a course on *Terry v. Ohio*. What is important about *Terry* is not in what year it occurred but what legal precepts it initiated for our profession. Issues like probable cause, custodial interrogation, and authority to frisk are the desired end products of what should be learned, not whether the case occurred in 1965, 1966, or 1968.*

---

* It may seem improbable that students would be tested on the year a landmark case was decided; however, this is often the case in many police academies. Test bank questions often ask for the student to recognize the proper year of a case in a multiple choice format. The real issue is that the performance objectives for constitutional law rarely (if ever) state that the student will identify the year of the case in question. Thus, the question is not validly tied to performance objectives and wholly inappropriate.

Although it may be interesting to present statistics, dates, and names, they must be relevant to your course in a meaningful way. If these references are immediately forgotten by learners, perhaps they are not truly important to what you are teaching. Instead, as instructors, we need to determine the underlying concepts within our content and how students can interact with and demonstrate their understanding of those concepts.

Students who cannot apply what you have taught them have learned nothing of value. Soliciting participation in a group activity or other constructed exercise substantially reinforces learning. These activities are not merely rote memorization drills but rather practice sessions of creative design that require the application of new skills and knowledge in a controlled setting.

Second, if you can allow students to practice the skills or apply their knowledge, they can assess the value of what they have just learned for themselves. Allowing students to participate in the process of their own education is a little-known secret in law enforcement training. During this kind of experience, the learner is compelled to participate in a self-analysis. Under these circumstances, if we could read the learner's mind, it might sound something like this:

Is this new information for me? If so, how does it affect my personal understanding or interpretation of _____?

Researchers in adult education know that it is not easy for adults to hear information that conflicts with their own foreknowledge of a topic. Encouraging this inner dialogue allows learners to make those critical connections between what they already knew or thought before your class and what they have just learned. Executed skillfully, students can then integrate this information into new patterns of knowing or thinking, after taking your class.

The first step to developing ancillary curriculum devices is to take a break from the development process after your content is complete. Give the new materials a rest for a week, without further revision or proofreading. Focus on another work project; catch up on your periodicals, research, or other demands. Then, when you are ready, revisit what content you have in hand and ask yourself this simple question: "So what?" How will this class affect the students in a meaningful way, and why should they attend it? Hopefully, you will be able to articulate an answer. This answer is the beginning to the process of ancillary development.

Using Exploratory Tasks

Exploratory tasks are those training exercises that allow the learner to determine what contents, points, and conclusions are relevant. Working with materials, students must use their own judgment and intellect to formulate an answer or defense, utilizing an example or direction provided by the instructor. In this way, learners cull through the material presented and answer the crucial question: What is important about this data to me?

A common application of this approach is seen in contemporary graduate degree programs. A professor asks a student to write a response to the following question:

> What constitutes use of excessive force by police officers?
> Discuss an example of a case known to you, whether by witness, participation, or media coverage.

The end result is usually an essay that will, hopefully, shed some light on the student's understanding on the topic and allow for a fruitful interaction between student and professor.

As police trainers, we have neither the desire nor time to assign such a writing assignment to our students. Although this kind of exercise encourages the kind of critical skill we want to cultivate, it is impractical and too far removed from the job of policing. We are not teaching some theory-based college course. Our training requires the development of skills that can be *applied*, not merely debated in the halls of educational institutions. Thus, we need a modified approach that preserves the intent of the exercise but replaces the theoretical aspects with real-world implications.

Rather than just tasking our students with essay-type questions, remember that active learning is needed. This need does not dictate that all of our objectives must become psychomotor — like shooting, driving, and fighting skills. Instead, it means that we must use our creativity to inject opportunities for student exploratory activity. By developing exercises that allow students to apply cognitive and affective skills in a practical way, we can encourage the critical thinking that police officers need in the field.

Let's examine the application of exploratory tasking on the topic of excessive force. You have defined the term for the students in the first fifteen minutes of class and now wish to gain their participation. One way of injecting life into the topic is to turn students loose in a computer lab with this fifteen-minute assignment:

> Find an example of the use of excessive force that was reported in the media. What are the facts of the case? Why was the force used considered excessive? Be prepared to brief your classmates on the background and current status of the case you select.

Students can be teamed in pairs or work independently. In this way, the learners control the development of their own understanding. There is an aspect of open-ended exploration as they seek out information that will meet your requirements. Once located, they must apply what you have taught them about excessive force to analyze a case for its content and meaning and then report their findings.* Will the students go to sleep in this class? It is highly doubtful.

Let's imagine that, like many police trainers, you have no access to resources like a computer lab for the students. How can you execute this kind of exercise without access to the Internet in the classroom? During your own research for the class development, you can locate and print out five different media stories on cases of excessive force. Place the students in small groups, hand out one story to each group, and task them with creating their response to the same questions. Ask the groups to report their findings in an open forum. In other words, you will prepare the data in advance and the students will analyze the value and content of the information you provide.

Students in police academies rarely, if ever, apply higher level cognitive skills during classroom training. This is because, by their very design and most of the time, our classroom training programs do not ask students to do, well, anything. The majority of the time, we lecture, reading slides to students and wondering why they intellectually drift away to more interesting thoughts, concerns, and dreams. Literally snowed under by weeks and months of mere talk, our students simply cannot hear us anymore. Exploratory tasks turn the traditional education model on its head. By making the student responsible for his own learning experience, we ask him to participate in his own education. We become the facilitators of knowledge, not merely the bearers of information. It is like the parable of the man who teaches the hungry villager how to fish instead of simply giving him a bucket of flounder. Our students must learn how to fish for themselves, and we can help them do it with exploratory tasks.

Developing Insightful Exercises

Imagine that you have developed a class that addresses the challenges of communicating with students across different generations. You have done your research and determined that there are ingrained, cultural identities of police trainees in "Generation Y" that are of potential interest to other trainers. You research and catalog ten different traits of the Gen Y recruit and come up with three approaches to bridging the communication gap. Excellent — you have finished your course outline. Once you convert your

---

* The performance objective for this activity is to analyze a media-reported incident of excessive force. This objective is a cognitive level four exercise, requiring analysis of facts by students. Contrast this level of functioning with the level one equivalent: define excessive force. Which objective creates more opportunity for interest and excitement?

outline to a completed lesson plan, your content is complete and ready for the ancillary process.

You take a week off from your materials and focus on other projects. Now, with a critical and open mind, you read your content and consider: "So what?" You will present all of this good information, but how will the trainers in your class *apply* this to their own work? You could leave it to them to figure out how to do this, once class ends. Up to 90 percent of police training classes ask this of their students. In all likelihood, the students will not undertake this process on their own and will probably forget what you have told them. However, if you can design an activity for students to engage in, you will see retention increase monumentally.

One option: develop a role-play. Divide students up into pairs. Have one learner play the role of trainer. The other learner, with a little preparation and assistance from you, will play the role of the Gen Y student. Trainers can be tasked with the following scenario:

Your current Gen Y recruit failed to conduct a thorough search of a prisoner, resulting in a missed weapon (knife). You will now conduct a remedial training session with him to counsel him about this incident. Keep in mind the principles of communicating with Gen Y recruits and apply them during this exercise.

In the opposite role, Gen Y role-players can gather in the hall, where they can be briefed privately about how to play their characters. For example, you might give them a brief outline of how to display Gen Y behaviors during this exercise:

Roll your eyes when the trainer corrects or scolds you.
If asked to respond, say, "Whatever," OR, "In the academy, they said ..."
Get quietly sullen about being criticized, unless the trainer applies the
    lessons of this course when communicating with you.

Exercises like this one are, by their very design, constructed to allow a humorous yet realistic interaction. Humor paired with realism is the key. There is no doubt that the law enforcement audience will enjoy this exercise. In fact, they have done so, within various agencies in multiple states. This exercise epitomizes the balance between reflecting reality to a great enough degree that students can use humor to enjoy themselves in these roles, and learn to apply new skills in a safe environment.

Another route to the same destination can be discerned through the use of this question: How can my students apply this information to something job- (or life-) related? If you can create an exercise that allows students to use the information you have just taught them, you have succeeded in developing ancillary content. This challenge can be accomplished through many avenues, across all disciplines. Central to the process is the development of a key question or issue to pose to students for reflection. Here are some examples:

Ethics: "Which behaviors would you tolerate from another officer before contacting internal affairs?"

In this example, you can challenge assumptions about the truth of working with police officers. Is there a true black-and-white ethics code for officers, or do we merely work in shades of grey? Which way is better?

Substance Abuse: "Can a police officer be both competent at his job and an alcoholic at the same time?"

This question elicits a natural uncertainty in the student. Perhaps an officer can be an alcoholic and still do the job, as long as he can keep the two separated. Or can he?

Officer Survival: "Should officers be prepared to use a tactical folding knife against a suspect in a deadly force confrontation?"

Most of our deadly force training is centered on the use of firearms. In this example, students will face the unexpected realization that they might have to hurt or kill someone in an up-close and personal way. Moreover, is it wrong for a police officer to use all available tools to survive — even tools like knives? This question plants the seed for surviving a worst-case scenario.

Recruitment: "What personal grooming standards should officers have to meet to wear the badge?"

This question allows a variety of different directions. How many tattoos are reasonable for a recruit to have? Should recruits with gang tattoos be excluded from consideration? What if they have renounced their gang membership or were merely "wannabes" to begin with? Should we allow police officers to wear unusual hairstyles, like muttonchop sideburns or cornrows? Why or why not?

Spend the hours you have during development to construct a like-minded exercise or interaction. Make your activity relevant to your topic but with a nod to a humorous or unusual aspect. Have students participate independently or interact in pairs. When time is short, instead have students practice in larger groups of four to six people. Although less participation can be had in a group of this size, it is still a good experience for students.

Right and Wrong Examples

At times, you may find that classes are too replete with crucial content to allow a significant addition of class time for an exercise. If this appears true for your particular course, look very closely at the content you have. If it is mostly lecture based, be concerned. If it solely uses a slide show to support instruction, be *extremely* concerned. Classes of two hours or more that do not include other methods of instruction, like break-out exercises, facilitated discussions, hands-on props, videos, or more creative means are doomed to mediocrity. Adults cannot sit and listen to an instructor teach for this period of time and maintain a high level of excitement and personal investment in the material. Unless you are among the lucky few who are phenomenal presenters, you will put your class to sleep with your aggregated, dry content.

Do not allow the lecture content of your classes to slowly kill students' interest in the topic at hand. Be more adventurous and figure out how to make small changes that will produce big results. If you have looked critically at what you have and determined that there is little room for the addition of alternate instructional methods due to time restraints, then incorporate short right and wrong drills to emphasize the student's development of judgment. For police training, especially, students want to apply what they know immediately. Give them this opportunity by crafting right and wrong examples, presenting them to the students, and asking for their input.

Imagine that you are teaching a course in interview and interrogation techniques. On the specific topic of obtaining a confession from a suspect, how could you employ right and wrong examples to enhance the interactive quality of your class? By the seat of your pants, it would be difficult to develop good right and wrong examples beyond your own limited experience. However, if you were to access one of several law Web sites and input the keyword "confession" or "suppressed confession," you would likely find a plethora of examples to use in your class based on case law.*

Let's examine one of these cases more closely and apply what we can to our imaginary course on confessions. In *Mincey v. Arizona* (1978), the Supreme Court ruled that the characteristics of a suspect were highly important when deciding whether a statement of confession is voluntary. In this case, Mincey was suspected as the shooter of an undercover police officer; he was shot during the fracas that ensued at the scene of the crime. Mincey was taken to the hospital where he was admitted to the intensive care unit

---

* Many case law citations can literally stretch into hundreds of pages. However, the better Web sites for case law references provide a concise, one- or two-paragraph summary of the facts of the case. These are excellent starting points for law enforcement curriculum development.

because of his injuries. Despite his condition, investigators conducted a relentless interrogation of Mincey while he was in the hospital, resulting in his confession. The confession was suppressed because of the suspect's condition — barely conscious, in the hospital, asking for a lawyer and refused one by the investigators.

Now, you have educated yourself about this case and understand it. How can you apply the lessons learned in this case to your ancillary course development? Envision your options as the function of two intersecting values: knowledge and interaction. Option one: lecture. Simply tell the students about the case. This choice is high on the knowledge scale but low on the interaction scale. It is the most common choice made by instructors who have quality information they want to teach. Unfortunately, it is an uninspired option. Lecture is a passive activity for the students and thus not as effective as we would like.

Option two: separate students into two groups to debate about the case findings. After telling the students the whole story, one group is assigned to argue in favor of the decision; the other group will argue against the decision. A high level of interaction occurs but perhaps at the expense of knowledge transmission. Students may not agree with what they must defend. They may also not be educated enough about the issues at hand to put their intellectual capacity to best use. After all, they are taking your class for a reason.

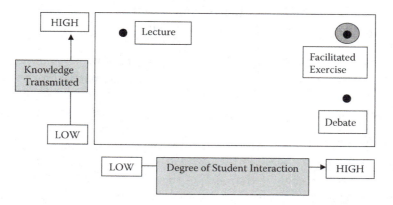

The best option: a facilitated exercise that allows the instructor to teach what "is" and the students will decide what "matters." Give the students the scenario in a dramatic and interesting way. You can select a skit or role-play approach as one choice. Do this by standing up students to represent the players in the drama. For example, Recruit A is the undercover officer, who is killed at the scene. Recruit B is the suspect, who is shot. Recruit C is the investigator who goes to the hospital to interrogate the suspect. This stand-up exercise can be as detailed as you like. You can call the shots through a detailed script, like a play, or adjourn to the hallway, brief the role-players, and tell them to create their own dialogue in three minutes or less.

Barring the overtly dramatic approach, you could relate the story in a "What if this happened to you?" kind of storytelling. Drawing on your creative side, you could allow this story to unfold in such a way that the students will have strong opinions about the players. For example, you could tell them that the suspect is somewhat cooperative, but "obviously guilty" and ask them:

How far would you go to get this confession?

Another option: have students analyze the case in a small group setting. You could write up a synopsis of six cases, leaving a mystery for the students to solve as to whether the confessions are legal or coerced. In this way, discovery is a highly engaging activity. Whether they end up being right or wrong in their opinions, students will appreciate the opportunity to contribute something to the learning experience.

Conclusion

Inside every police student is an amateur attorney. Most cops have an interest in the law or they would not be in the criminal justice field. When tasking students with judgment-based activities surrounding case law, police officers in training will be interested in what the facts are and what occurred as a result of those facts. They will want to know the end of the story, if you can prepare them for the intellectual journey at hand. In our imaginary course on interview and interrogation, this means which confessions were legitimate and which were not. The interest of students is not a chance occurrence. They will develop interest through active participation in cleverly designed exercises.

I highly recommend small groups for these types of activities because interaction increases retention. When you are truly pressed for time, still allow students to recognize the value of the information presented through the use of right and wrong examples. Why does this technique work? The answer is because it allows police trainees to *work with* information and not simply *hear about it* in a lecture or *watch it* in a video. Case law is an excellent raw material for developing these kinds of exercises. Another source is the news media and listservs for criminal justice professionals.

Instructors must have an understanding of the need to cultivate a two-way relationship with the learner, not simply to be the cardboard cutout reading a script at the podium. Students who are encouraged to participate through facilitation, positive regard, and true intellectual engagement have a reason to remember what they have just learned. Through the use of careful ancillary development, you will give students the opportunity to apply their internal cognitive and affective processes in a new way. By encouraging interaction between and with students, you can increase the quality of your results in the classroom.

In the end, the best training challenges assumptions, particularly those based on a student's ill-wrought conjectures or their long-held, erroneous beliefs. Top-notch trainers allow this dialogue to take place in the classroom, while they can still facilitate further understanding of the topic in the classroom setting. I challenge you to remember that the student is the reason for the training session and teach accordingly.

Current and Future Trends in Police Training

14

It is not reasonable that those who gamble with men's lives should not stake their own.

—H.G. Wells

If we could climb into a time machine, like a character from one of Wells' novels, we could see the inevitable results of increasing technology applications to law enforcement training in the coming years. Although Wells' quote specifically refers to politicians, it applies to our trainers of police officers as well. What other profession can be so ripe with sacrifice and personal danger, so genuinely thankless, and yet so compellingly satisfying and critical to preserving the delicate boundaries of society as police work?

As we have always been, police officers are still the last line of defense between criminals and the innocent civilians they prey on. As trainers of police, we have the imperative task of preparing new officers to survive, nay even thrive, on the stressful diet of shift work, crummy take-out food, gut-wrenching crime scenes, criminal shenanigans and, often, overt public rejection. Unlike politicians, 99.9 percent of police trainers take their jobs seriously and recognize the deep responsibilities with which we are tasked. So, given this burden, how will new technologies arm us for coping with the next generation of recruits?

In this chapter, we will examine some emerging training trends and their potential impact on police training. Already, the increased use of scenario-based training and virtual reality technology seem poised to completely outpace and overtake classroom instruction in the near future. The advent of e-learning systems and the resulting explosion of self-instruction and individually paced training programs may render obsolete the need for converging traditional classes that are bound by space and time constraints. Eventually, it will no longer be necessary to contact a supervisor to come to a scene. They will be channeled via technology. Officers can be supervised from within the station, by sergeants who sit at a control console with access to streaming Webcams, inset inconspicuously within the officer's uniform lapel.

As a profession, what improvements will technology offer us from a training perspective? Certainly, training and supervision costs will be lower over time, as fewer instructor-led courses are utilized. The front-end development costs, in terms of manpower and technology, can be quite high. But, in the end, will we be able to retain the crucial personal connections with law enforcement students, when virtually all of our training is outsourced to an e-learning format? Let's examine the emerging changes for training police in the coming decades, with an open mind and a critical eye.

Scenario-Based Learning

Scenario-based learning (SBL) has fantastic applications for law enforcement training and is a welcome addition to any trainer's toolbox. Essentially, SBL allows students to take on the role of police officers, practicing motor skills and applying higher level thinking and affective skills in a safe environment. Students act more or less independently of instructor direction, make judgment calls, and engage in detailed role-playing in realistic environments.

In its current form, SBL is well regarded. Trainees wholeheartedly report high levels of enthusiasm and interest in SBL exercises, and instructors find that student behaviors seen during SBL are viable indicators of overall student competency, across a range of skills. Through the conduct of a "hot-wash" immediately after the module ends, instructors can question recruits about their actions (or inactions) and elucidate key teaching points. This on-the-spot correction that occurs immediately after SBL ends is the closest thing to field training officer (FTO) training that recruits will get in the academy.

The typical SBL application is structured in a somewhat open-ended fashion. SBL modules are designed by instructors in advance, with (hopefully) a clear outline of what events will happen under which circumstances. Locales are chosen. Props and weapons are included (or hidden) within the scene as required. Role-players are briefed as to the rules and parameters of their roles. Ideally, SBL grading is tied directly to student performance objectives from an existing curriculum.

Generally, students enter the scenario after a short briefing or by responding to a call for service. Often, SBL is conducted on a rotation, where students are paired as partners and move from one SBL module to the next, over a period of several hours or days.

A briefing is given to the students to provide some indication of what scenario is likely to unfold. For example:

> You have arrived at the scene of a reported burglary of a business. The owner, Joe Blow, told the dispatcher he will meet you outside the business. He reported that he is wearing a blue jogging suit.

Wily instructors like to mix up the action to keep the scenario "fresh," given these circumstances. Perhaps there will be no owner at the scene — only a suspect who attempts to fool the officers with some slick double-talk. Or, the owner might be *inside* the business and the officers would be expected to verbally challenge the owner at gunpoint before deescalating to a field interview. Another alternative: the owner is outside the business, but he is *not* wearing a blue jogging suit. Yet another iteration of this module might call for an owner to be held at gunpoint by the suspect, who must be "talked down" from executing the owner (or himself).

The training results of these kinds of SBL exercises can be, at times, unpredictable. Recruits may not recognize the subtle signs of deception that we expect them to notice. Novice officers may be so "keyed up" with adrenaline that they shoot participants before they can even question them in the scenario.* Depending on the training they have been given, some recruits may be totally unprepared for conducting actual interviews. Likewise, recruits may try to "pause" the action, mid-scenario, so they may ask questions or seek direction from the instructor about what to do next.

On the instructor side, these kinds of SBL exercises can also be fraught with perils. We run the risk of conducting a seat-of-the-pants operation when we do not expect the same skills for each set of students. If Recruit A fails to manage the slick-talking suspect who masquerades as the owner, but Recruit B handles a hostage negotiation within the same scenario, are we using the same yardstick to measure each student's performance? I think not. The consequences for failure to execute fair and equitable training standards for all recruits can result in a training liability outcome that is particularly undesirable — a lawsuit.

An even worse outcome can occur when poorly structured SBL modules result in physical injuries to role-players, instructors, and recruits. Overzealous actors can occasionally act dangerously, under the guise of "realistic" training. In 2002, I watched a certified defensive tactics trainer conduct a spontaneous SBL with his students, donning Red-Man® gear and asking students to "take their best shot" at controlling him with empty-handed techniques.† One student was knocked briefly unconscious after being choked out by the instructor. A second student sustained a torn rotator cuff in his shoulder after being flung backwards by the instructor, who had obviously thrown caution to the wind during this exercise. The former student had no lasting damage from the event; the latter returned to training after shoulder surgery and several months of rehabilitation. This kind of training has no place in a professional training academy. Do not use SBL as an excuse to

---

* Obviously, SBL is not safely conducted with live weapons of any kind. Simunitions® marking ammunition or other inert training weapons may be used in simulated deadly force encounters.

† Florida-based Red-Man® is a great training tool that allows trainers to wear protective gear in order to minimize injuries and allow students to replicate a realistic —fifty to seventy percent strength strike to green, yellow, and red zones. This event relates a misuse of a great tool and in no way implies a shortcoming with using Red-Man products.

"rough up" students who are still incredibly new to the profession of policing. Instructor-supervised safety protocols are extremely important.

For jurisdictions who are not yet conducting SBL on a regular basis, it is the future of the profession. The most important consideration in developing SBL is safety. It is crucial to have established safety guidelines that are known to all persons involved in the scenario. It is especially important to control the behavior of the role-players, as opposed to the actions of the students. Role-players must be willing to conform to the rules set out by instructors or they cannot participate in SBL in a productive way. The student briefing should include an "out of role" directive: When the instructor barks, "Out of role," all action will cease *immediately*. Instructors who proctor SBL exercises must control the action at all times and call "Out of role" when players are at risk of harming themselves or others.

Writing SBL Objectives

Under the best circumstances, SBL is dynamic by design. It reinforces the lessons learned during classroom instruction through the opportunity for hands-on practice. It is during SBL that it becomes apparent whether classroom learning objectives are tied to realistic, police-oriented job tasks. For example, consider the following:

> Objective: Understand the importance of communicating effectively with a victim of a burglary.

Understanding the importance of the skill is not the same as being able to actually do it. Likewise, knowing that communication is important and being able to actually communicate are two very different things. Poorly written student performance objectives cannot be measured during SBL or, empirically, in any other valid way. This is an irrelevant objective. We must return to the question of what we want the student to be able to say, do, or show at the end of the course.

> Revised Objective: During SBL, demonstrate effective communication with a victim of a burglary by gathering basic information for a police report, including victim's name, address, and telephone number.

When utilizing SBL, it is recommended that trainers write a detailed plan to establish the different potential versions of each scenario that will be acceptable within each module. Consult your objectives first. Know what skills you are assessing, and ensure that those skills are the targets of each possible scenario.

For example, if the scenario is supposed to assess the ability of the student to communicate with the victim as described in the above objective, these options might be possible:

Scenario: Burglary I
> Role-Player 1: You are the owner of the business that has been burglarized. At the direction of the instructor, you will act in the following way:
> - Be polite. Answer the questions and be very accommodating to the officer.
> - Be defensive. Show that you are suspicious of the police and not very confident that they will find the culprit.
> - Be belligerent. Talk angrily to the officer and blame him for your current situation. You will not take any physical action against the officer.

Notice how the scenario remains essentially unchanged. It does not spontaneously transmogrify into a hostage negotiation or other vastly different encounter. The students will still have to demonstrate the same communication skills and gather the right information, but the traits of the interviewee may change, depending on the circumstances.

A Model of Excellence: Howard County, Maryland

SBL is a tool that is best used to achieve defined goals of student performance under controlled conditions. It has tremendous applications for the future. In some places, like Howard County, Maryland, the police academy has already taken SBL to the next level through the use of intricately rendered SBL buildings. Completed in 2008, Howard County's new SBL facility is among the best in the country, rivaling those of many federal agencies in terms of its scope, design, and size. Specific corridors, both outside and indoor, are fitted with integrated audio and video technology to capture all of the action. SBL sessions can be recorded for later student debriefing and archived indefinitely.

Students enter scenarios under the watchful eyes of instructors who view their performance from behind one-inch-thick glass. Inside observation areas that have been installed adjacent to the SBL rooms, instructors can watch the events impartially, from a safe distance. The self-contained, fully compartmentalized scenario rooms have closets, kitchens, and bathrooms, complete with furniture, utensils, fake plants, and artwork on the walls. There are dedicated, SBL-ready apartments, hotel rooms, townhouses with multiple floors, banks, and an auto-body shop. Several special buildings are designated for tactical entry training, using a ram and fast rope-rappel-ling techniques. The wealth of possibilities that this kind of training facility inspires is beyond measure.

In the future of law enforcement training, SBL will become the showpiece of effective instruction. All training will culminate with scenario-driven opportunities for students. Increasingly realistic backdrops will allow the use of a range of strategies and weapons by students during SBL — from empty-hand techniques and take-downs to chemical weapons deployment and Simunition® rounds. The absence of the perpetually hovering instructor at the side of the students will add to the independent feel of scenarios, as trainers use integrated technology to evaluate students.

Police trainers who have had the opportunity to participate in well-designed SBL know its value as the incumbent "gold standard" in train-ing design. SBL offers students a realistic taste of police work that is as close to live action as possible without potentially placing students on the street. In the future, the use of SBL will only increase as the results of this dynamic level of training become evident to police executives.

Virtual Reality

Virtual reality (VR) technology is the future version of SBL and is on the cusp of breakthrough applications for training. I foresee a time when stu-dents can suit up and enter a world where they can practice psychomotor skills on virtual suspects under extremely realistic conditions. Imagine being able to provide a truly immersive experience for students, who enter a tech-nology-powered world like Keanu Reeve's "Neo" in the movie *The Matrix*. The higher the degree of perfection that VR technology achieves, the greater the resulting implications will be for revolutionary new training products, for all fields.

Imagine survival training with computer-imposed consequences. Fighting through combat "injuries" would become possible, simulated by actual physical sensations of injury. Induced "tunnel vision" simulations could be trained through, based on computerized tracking of the player's eye movements during deadly force events. A variety of opponents for physical confrontations with varying levels of pain tolerance and technical fighting expertise could be designed within the VR platform. Opponents who bleed, punch, curse, and bite could be programmed to learn to defend against your favorite defensive tactics techniques over time. Fighting simulations could provide a range of targeted pain "feedback" when a player is struck with a blow, whether in his arms, legs, or face, through nerve stimulation.

There may be more than thirty years' wait for these unbelievable pos-sibilities, but they are likely to emerge one day, made possible through technologies that we have today. Some of us may live to see their implementation and perhaps even suit up ourselves, one day. Until then, SBL gives us the opportunity to provide the greatest degree of realism for students today.

E-Learning and Computer-Based Training

Anyone who has even taken a computer-based training (CBT) course has an opinion about the quality of the product they used. Characterized by point-and-click, often with frustrating question-and-answer sessions to gauge your level of attention, CBT is not warmly welcomed by law enforcement. Many of these courses are dry, uninspired depictions of training at its very worst. With the idea that CBT courses free up funds and make learning more accessible to all, administrators are increasingly embracing these kinds of e-learning programs for all manner of training.

How can e-learning be made dynamic for the student? It cannot be done without technological savvy. Trainers who must now develop e-learning for police officers must keep in mind that the audience is not interested in mundane, stereotypical, canned presentations. The slide show format of most e-learning courses is not going to inspire any excitement in this profession.

E-learning can be enhanced with interactive features, but unless it is visually appealing, the experience is less than enjoyable most of the time. Embedded video, audio, and other items can enhance training, but often police officers just want to get the training over with by fast-forwarding through anything that is not absolutely mandatory.

However, exceptions to the boredom rule do exist. I recently experienced a refreshing approach in the form of a computer security course I took online in 2009. The course was structured as a series of mini-games with engaging, high-quality graphics. First, the player is informed that she is to take on the role of a thieving employee working inside an office building. The building is shown as a large skyscraper with six cut-away depictions of offices. The player is then asked to choose an office. Each office holds a different scenario.

In one office, the graphics show a cluttered desk, complete with a dying potted plant, computer screen, papers, and office cabinets. The resolution is cartoon-like but high quality and equivalent to a typical video game. The player then reads and hears:

Helen has hidden her password in what she thinks is a safe place while she is gone to lunch. Click on different locations in her desk and see if you can find Helen's password.

The player then clicks on Helen's desk drawers, file cabinet, and other items. Each click reveals a short tidbit of security training. Clicking on the trash can reveals: "The trash is a place many people believe is secure. Shred any information you wouldn't want others to read." Once the password is "stolen," the player is told to write this password down and proceed to one of the other offices to "steal" more items. Later, he will use his espionage to commit a "security breach" and, thereby, complete the training.

This kind of format is interactive, fun, and engaging for players. They learn about security through the use of right and wrong interactive examples. Online programs like this make e-learning dynamic, interesting, and well worth the investment. As police trainers, we should take a clue from the hugely successful gaming industry.

Gaming

Can games be used to effectively teach police officers skills? I suggest that the answer is an unequivocal, yes. Plus, they offer an entertainment factor for the participant. Let's consider, for example, an old-fashioned board game: chess. What kinds of skills are learned from moving rooks and pawns around a checkered board? Chess players learn the importance of strategy, risk, consequences, and planning as they engage more skilled players. As they play, they learn to ask themselves: What significance does this particular move, at this particular time by my opponent, have in the overall context of the game? Chess reinforces these kinds of thinking skills beyond the game itself and into real-life applications for players. Ask any chess player: the game has far more value than simply a bit of fun.

Now, let's examine a more contemporary computer-based gaming format. Sims, short for simulations, are virtual environments that respond to player's actions. In one type of Sim, the role-playing game (RPG), players navigate through medieval quests, complex combat, business ventures, even love, marriage, and parenting. Most tech-savvy people realize that incredibly sophisticated RPG worlds exist online today, with literally millions of faithful players. Indeed, perhaps some police trainers are familiar with these RPGs as players themselves.

What, if anything, do these games teach? First, they allow the controlled use of fantasy in a safe environment. For example, players can choose to be good or evil, magicians or barbarians, and be fair or cheat without compromising their "real" lives. Games allow people to act out their desires in a relatively benign way. Second, they teach valuable communication skills. Players can provoke or persuade characters and experience the consequences of their actions. Last, they learn strategy. As players interact with computer-generated worlds, virtual and human players, and various foes, they learn strategies for survival, cooperation, a degree of interdependence, and successful planning. Are these not the same skills that we want police officers to learn?

With the right technological expertise, nothing should stop us from developing high-quality RPGs for police training in the future. Through gaming, police recruits could learn a tremendous amount of information about policies, practices, and procedures. Learners would take charge of their own education, using carefully designed products that teach identified skills.

For example, imagine an RPG created for patrol work. In this RPG, the player must articulate radio responses to calls, navigate a patrol car through the streets, and approach and manage a variety of scenes. We could interject ethical dilemmas, report writing, arrests, and field interviews. An encounter with the sergeant could spell "game over" if a player has neglected his duties or made a "bad" arrest.

Through an automated process, students would successfully complete their gaming "assignment" by scoring an eighty-five percent (or whatever standard) on the given Sim. Student scores could be collected and reported to trainers via an online collection system. Trainers could analyze performance for factors such as time spent in a given Sim, number of plays by the student before achieving success, use of interviewing skills, and ethical decisions made during the Sim. Then, trainers could provide targeted remediation for areas of weakness identified.

With some creativity and technological know-how, police trainers could become the newest masterminds of gaming, designing products specifically for law enforcement training. Obviously, we need talented graphics designers, programmers, and creative minds to envision such a product, but the potential is virtually limitless. Gaming is the future of training in essential skills, and students will enjoy the opportunities that games will provide.

Conclusion

Consider the tremendous strides in technology that have been made in the life of the common man in the past thirty years. The proliferation of personal computers, handheld electronic communications devices, e-mail access, vehicle airbags, and commercialized plastics are no small feature of our lives today. In 2010, we are in a completely different universe than our parents' generation. The same will be true of police training environments, thirty years from now.

With the advent of SBL, police instructors have one of the best measures of student readiness for graduation onto the streets. Executed well, SBL is highly realistic, dynamic, and directly tied to performance objectives for students. When ill-planned, SBL is dangerously unstructured and totally invalid for assessing student competencies. Using SBL with strict guidelines and planning, trainers will be able to see a range of skills demonstrated by students in a safe environment.

The future application of virtual reality to the field of law enforcement training will have far-reaching implications. Simulated line-of-duty events could be designed to impress upon students the importance of the goals of officer survival training. A creative employment of gaming as a possible training tool should not be underestimated as "pop" science. Gaming is an engaging and interactive method of training others and will have wide application in the coming years as it becomes embraced by many professions, including law enforcement.

It is an exciting time to be involved with police training. As new technology emerges, trainers must find the specific applications for our work and use them judiciously. A diligent appreciation for what is possible in the future of teaching police officers is needed by all trainers. When possible, acquire an education of your own to further your understanding of technology applications that can be utilized to serve the important needs of police officers.

Conclusion 15

There is plenty of room at the top because very few people care to travel beyond ... the confines of mediocrity.

—Nnamdi Azikiwe

Is there a destination beyond mediocrity for those who choose to pursue greatness? I believe that excellence in training, born out of study and experience, is possible because there is no limit to human potential. The resourcefulness of my colleagues has ever delighted and never failed to surprise me. As a group of people with an extremely heavy responsibility, police trainers are, unquestionably, diamonds in the rough. I am proud to be counted with my peers in the trenches of police training.

Sometimes, taking the road less traveled is the best option, within the realm of training and, indeed, life itself. As instructors, it is certainly our hope that this road will lead to better results, especially in the classroom. Too many of our opportunities to really affect students in a meaningful way are squandered unnecessarily. By employing a spoon-feeding approach to imparting knowledge using lecture, our students neither develop new skills nor change their own deep-seated mindsets while under our direction. They simply listen and forget. It is time for something better.

Historically, we are not far removed from old-fashioned approaches to police training. I see our profession as one in transition. In the end, the results of this dramatic metamorphosis will be grand, but getting there is not going to be easy. We trainers must adopt new approaches to adapt to these ever-increasing demands for highly trained police officers. Using adult learning principles specifically tailored for our profession, we can achieve the transformation we need and create dynamic classroom training every day. I believe that it is only a matter of speaking the language of police trainers, having walked in those close-fitting shoes.

Police administrators have not been very helpful in nurturing the delicate balance of expertise and passion required from us, the instructors of the next generation. We are all perpetually sidelined by bureaucratic memos and directives that seek to manage the endemic creative process of curriculum development and management on all fronts. In places where police instructors are not permitted to develop materials at all, the situation is even worse. Merely allowed to present the vetted lesson plans written by well-intentioned civilians, instructors who work under these circumstances are treated like mindless, automaton badge-wearers. They bring the needed credibility to the classroom but are barred from presenting legitimate police-oriented content, developed by cops and for cops. So, they fall back on their war stories and other underground means to transmit the essential lessons of police work. Yet, because of the lecture-heavy structure of our programs, these true kernels of wisdom are lost in the sea of unnecessary, continual commentary of classroom instruction.

It is not the instructors themselves who have failed; it is the system we have built for instructors that needs renovation. Sometimes, builders will tell you it is easier to tear down a shoddily built house than to renovate it. The degree of frustration you may feel with a careful examination of an existing program may be completely outshined by your perfect vision and enthusiasm about what the program can be. Using the tools in this book, you may be able to institute some changes in your programs. By educating yourself on how to instruct smarter and how to develop well-designed, active programs for law enforcement that encourage thought, feeling, and movement, perhaps you can take back some of the responsibility for the results in the classroom.

The methods of this book do require a commitment, of both time and self-examination, in terms of preparation and careful selection of materials. Make no mistake — it is not an overnight process. Perhaps new habits may be needed — habits of research, collaboration with peers, and quality control reviews. Instructor excellence is an evolving competency that generally improves with invested time and experience. When people work well together, these competencies grow exponentially. Investments in self-improvement are truly worthwhile endeavors that can be measured in concrete results. I can assure you that witnessing the experiences of students through dynamic training programs is its own self-affirming, perpetual reward.

In the final analysis, recognize that it matters less what you write in your lesson plans than the content of your overall teaching character. Guided by humility, personal courage, and positive regard for others, almost anything is possible. Although lesson plan formats strive to make instruction more uniform and neat, do not become a prisoner to format over function. If the spontaneous nature of your instruction suffers when tied to lesson plans, do not marry yourself to using them. Teach with passion and ask for help from others in the translation of that passion to paper. Allow another instructor to attend your class as a note-taking observer; he can provide you with the framework for the lesson plan as the instruction was truly rendered in the class.

Understand that there are vast differences in people, across cultural, gender, and age boundaries. Instructors who can learn to appreciate, and even welcome, discord are among those teachers counted in legends. When a facilitator can take the time to acknowledge and respect the learning preferences in every classroom, it is nothing less than a magical experience. Thus, I understand, my neighbors understand, and we all experience spontaneous growth as people, standing in the sunlight of new ideas. We become better people when we can experience that extraordinary combination of education, affirmation, and insight. It is like harnessing a lightning bolt when you can affect people so deeply and directly, through teaching.

Dare to dream of nontraditional approaches to training. Some of the best ideas are borne out of so-called crazy musings. Do not be afraid to try a new role-play, an unproven exercise, or a completely different perspective on an old topic. Students enjoy surprises in the classroom, especially when the surprise is not another lecture. Assuming that you do not compromise safety considerations, no permanent damage will be done through experimentation. The future holds great promise for sights and experiences yet unseen. Keep yourself informed about what others are doing and learning about, so that you can make your contribution to the new methods and applications of the coming years.

The book you hold in your hands is but one starting place for improving instructor skills. There are many, many better written, better researched, and more eloquently finished books. However, you will not find one book that is more certainly the product of a passionate, ambitious vision of how police training might be. At least, this is my understanding of the work I have tried to represent here. It remains for the reader to determine whether *Dynamic Police Training* has any inherent value, beyond that of a rather expensive paperweight.

This book includes a modest curriculum development template that can be used in your own training creation endeavors, contained in the Appendix. Use these forms to inspire your own creativity and flesh out ideas to set the stage for a more dynamic presentation on topics of your choice. As you use these forms, remember that the goal is not to merely entertain students but to create orchestrated "lightning" moments of comprehension for students. Connecting a student's past experience with today's lessons is so crucial to making a training difference. The key to these moments is the interactive nature of teaching, allowing students to work with information and skills, which I have tried to detail in this book. Creating a systematic approach to including interaction as a preferred choice is the aim of these templates.

It is my sincere hope that, as you sharpen your skills, you can create more of these lightning moments, as I have been honored to experience over the years. Never forget: Instruction is a sacred role that must not be taken for granted. Along with the privilege of parenthood, teaching is among one of the most singularly meaningful experiences life has to offer. Give your students the best of yourself in all things and, thus, inspire them to greatness by example.

Appendix

Materials

Curriculum Development Template: Part I

Working Title of Course:

Select all that apply:

- ☐ I want students to develop knowledge about my topic. [C]
- ☐ I want students to feel/understand the importance/relevance of my topic. [A]
- ☐ I want student to learn a hands-on skill in my class. [P]

[C] = Cognitive skills   [A] = Affective skills   [P] = Psychomotor skills

Objectives: Circle your choice of verbs. At the end of this course, the student will:

[C]	[A]	[P]
Define	Share	Respond to
Identify	Discuss the importance of	Prepare for
Compare	Participate	Simulate
Describe	Contribute	Demonstrate
Prepare	Appreciate	Hear
Relate	Report	Draw
Explain	Debate	Locate
Propose	Generalize	Troubleshoot
Recommend	Revise	Control
Select	Avoid	Restore
Estimate	Resolve	Operate
Develop	Specify	Apply

Curriculum Development Template: Part II

Objective ___ of _____ (use one sheet per objective)

Circle the domain: [C]   [A]   [P]

Write the objective: At the end of this course, the student will _____

_____

_____.

Content: Consider the following items.

A. How can I make this particular objective interesting for learners?
   - ☐ Surprising statistics/facts   ☐ Humor
   - ☐ Dramatic storytelling   ☐ Other _____

B. How is this particular objective relevant to an officer's day-to-day work?
   - ☐ Survival oriented   ☐ Makes student smarter/faster/better
   - ☐ Real consequences of failure   ☐ Other _____

C. Aside from a slide show, what visual technique will I use for this objective?
   - ☐ Pictures/photos   ☐ Video
   - ☐ Handouts   ☐ Other _____

D. Aside from a lecture, what auditory technique will I use for this objective?
   - ☐ Video w/audio   ☐ Discussion
   - ☐ Dramatic storytelling   ☐ Other _____

E. What kinesthetic (hands-on) technique will I use for this objective?
   - ☐ Handouts requiring activity   ☐ Props/equipment
   - ☐ Student/group practice session   ☐ Other _____

F. Which questions can I ask of the students that relate to this objective?
   - ☐ "What would happen if … ?"   ☐ "Can anyone tell me … ?"
   - ☐ "Who has had an experience … ?"   ☐ Other _____

Research Source 1:   Internet   Book   News Article   Magazine   Other
Name/Web Address: _____
Author/Publisher: _____
Key info: _____
_____

Research Source 2:   Internet   Book   News Article   Magazine   Other
Name/Web Address: _____
Author/Publisher: _____
Key info: _____
_____

Research Source 3:   Internet   Book   News Article   Magazine   Other
Name/Web Address: _____
Author/Publisher: _____
Key info: _____
_____

Curriculum Development Template: Part III

Introduction of self: What will I tell students about myself in 60 seconds or less?

Introduction to topic or A/Set: What is an interesting, ironic, or dramatic opening for this topic? Do NOT simply list objectives here.

Making it interactive: What techniques will I use in addition to a lecture and slide show? Select one or more of the following:

- ☐ Ice-breaker. Limit to 10, 15, or 30 minutes.
- ☐ Brainstorm. What question(s) can I pose for students to provide input on?
- ☐ Case study. Which infamous, personal, or media-reported cases can I use?
- ☐ Demonstration. Who can assist me in the live demo?
- ☐ Role-playing. Can I show right and/or wrong examples?
- ☐ Skits. What is the central idea or lesson of the skit I will present?
- ☐ Group exercise. What bones of contention will I use for group work?
- ☐ Scenario-based learning environment. What safety guidelines are important?
- ☐ Other _____

Conclusion: List the most important relevant points that were taught in this course. Do NOT simply list objectives here.

Selected Bibliography

Bloom B. S. *Taxonomy of Educational Objectives, Handbook I: The Cognitive Domain.* New York: David McKay Co., Inc., 1956.

Blum, L. *Force under Pressure.* New York: Lantern Books, 2000.

Cole, R. *Under the Gun in Iraq.* New York: Prometheus Books, 2007.

Covey, S. *Seven Habits of Highly Effective People.* New York: Free Press, 1990.

Covey, S. *First Things First.* New York: Fireside, 1994.

Foy, D. *Treating PTSD.* New York: Guilford Press, 1992.

Kirschman, E. *I Love a Cop.* New York: Guilford Press, 1997.

Kiyosaki, R. *Rich Dad, Poor Dad.* New York: Hachette Group, 1997.

Luttrell, M. *Lone Survivor.* New York: Hachette Group, 2007.

Marcinko, R. and J. Weisman. *Rogue Warrior: Red Cell.* New York: Simon & Schuster, 1994.

Marcinko, R. and J. Weisman. *Rogue Warrior: Task Force Blue.* New York: Simon & Schuster, 1996.

Marcinko, R. and J. Weisman. *Rogue Warrior: Detachment Bravo.* New York: Simon & Schuster, 2001.

Maryland Police and Correctional Training Commissions. *Enhanced Instructor Training Manual.* Baltimore: Maryland, 2008.

Parsons, D. and P. Jesilow. *In the Same Voice.* Santa Ana, CA: Seven Locks Press, 2001.

Schwarz, R. *The Skilled Facilitator.* San Francisco: Jossey-Bass, 2002.

Siddle, B. *Sharpening the Warrior's Edge.* Chicago: PPCT Research Publications, 1995.

Wilson, J., M. Friedman, and J. Lindy, Eds. *Treating Psychological Trauma and PTSD.* New York: Guilford Press, 2001.

Index